UNCOVER THE AUTHENTIC YOU

Many women view middle age as a watershed from which all roads lead downhill ... to wrinkles, cellulite, widowhood, and invisibility.

Though all midlifers must undergo some identity reformation, this time presents unique challenges to the Superwoman, who, at some time in her early development, began to nurture the more masculine aspects of herself.

Superwomen often approach midlife feeling burned out, bewildered, and betrayed.

For years, they have overextended their bodies, minds, hearts, and souls to create and to maintain an inauthentic idenity—one that has systematically ignored or demeaned the very core of who they really are.

SuperWoman's Rite of Passage redefines midlife as an opportunity to rebuild your identity, to bring your whole self into being, and to become real—with yourself and others.

This is a time to seek out new sources of strength and support. Through the help of this interactive guidebook, you will:

- Awaken your natural feminine gifts of intuition, wisdom, creativity, and spirituality
- Return to the roots of your womanly competence
- Go forth in life with newly-acquired authenticity, autonomy, and authority

SuperWoman's Rite of Passage will help you locate limitless sources of energy and inspiration. You will learn to use nature and myth as unwavering guideposts throughout your midlife transition and beyond.

About the Author

Kathleen Lundquist holds a doctorate from the College of Education, University of Minnesota. As a transformational teacher with over twenty-five years of experience, she has worked with students between the ages of three and eighty-three, in the United States, Canada, and Spain. As a young widow and single parent, Kathleen co-founded the Minnesota Center for Grief and Loss, for which she received an Outstanding Leadership Award from the Minnesota Division of the American Cancer Society. Currently, Kathleen models her deep commitment to service and lifelong learning in parenting her teenage daughter, practicing meditation and Tai Chi Chih, writing nonfiction, and operating Crossroads, an educational consulting firm that focuses on issues related to the spirituality of aging at midlife and beyond.

To Write to the Author

If you wish to contact the author or would like more information about this book, please write to the author in care of Llewellyn Worldwide, and we will forward your request. Both the author and publisher appreciate hearing from you and learning of your enjoyment of this book and how it has helped you. Llewellyn Worldwide cannot guarantee that every letter written to the author can be answered, but all will be forwarded. Please write to:

Llewellyn Worldwide Ltd.

P.O. Box 64383-K447, St. Paul, MN 55164-0383, U.S.A.

Please enclose a self-addressed, stamped envelope for reply, or $1.00 to cover costs.
If outside the U.S.A., enclose international postal reply coupon.

Free Catalog from Llewellyn

LLEWELLYN'S WHOLE LIFE SERIES

SuperWoman's
Rite of Passage

From Midlife to Whole Life

KATHLEEN LUNDQUIST, PH.D.

1996
LLEWELLYN PUBLICATIONS
ST. PAUL, MINNESOTA, 55164-0383, U.S.A.

FIRST EDITION, 1996
First Printing

Cover art and design by Anne Marie Garrison
Interior design and editing by Connie Hill

Library of Congress Cataloging-in-Publication Data
Lundquist, Kathleen F.
SuperWoman's rite of passage: from midlife to whole life / Kathleen F. Lundquist. — 1st ed.
p. cm. — (Llewellyn's whole life series:)
Includes bibliographical references and index.
ISBN 1-56718-447-2 (trade paperback)
1. Women—Religious life. 2. Women—Psychology. I. Title. II. Series.
BL625.7.L87 1996
291.4'4'082—dc20 95-47533
CIP

Llewellyn Publications
A Division of Llewellyn Worldwide, Ltd.
St. Paul, Minnesota, 55164-0383, U.S.A.

ABOUT LLEWELLYN'S WHOLE LIFE SERIES

Each of us is born into a body. But an amazing number of us lack anything beyond the most utilitarian connection with our physical beings. Yet, being "in touch" with the body—being aware of the senses' connection to our thoughts, emotions, dreams, and spirits—is integral to holistic living.

What does the physical have to do with the emotional or the spiritual? Everything. We are as much beings of the Earth as we are beings of the stars … our senses and connection to our bodies are just as integral to our physical, emotional, and spiritual well-being as is our connection to our higher selves.

The old doctrines, which regard the physical as inferior to the spiritual, may have made sense for the medieval ascetic—but, much like the medieval belief that the Sun orbited the Earth, those beliefs have been supplanted by more enlightened ones. Fortunately. Because it is impossible to truly feel that we belong in the universe, just as much as the ground we walk on and the air we breathe, until we entirely accept our own natures as physical and spiritual creatures. This book will help you heal the split between will and understanding and further your journey to wholeness, the place where body, mind, and spirit are integrated and healed. Access your internal source of wisdom, love, and healing through the techniques presented here for heightened mind and body awareness … and become so much more than the sum of your parts.

SuperWoman's Rite of Passage offers a model of transition for the high-achieving woman facing midlife crisis. Working through a five-step process of rebirth, women can uncover their feminine psyche and, along with it, a source of limitless enthusiasm and energy for the second half of life.

Other Books by the Author

Ethnic Variations in Death and Dying: Diversity in Universality. Co-written with D. Irish, and V. Jenkins Nelson, published by Taylor & Francis Pub., Inc., 1993.

Kids Count, Too: A Grief Curriculum for Children Three to Twelve. Co-written with L. Norquist, published by American Cancer Society–MN Division, 1989.

To Eileen, Steve, and Frankie, whose combined knowledge and skills helped me remember and embrace the reality of my True Self.

ACKNOWLEDGEMENTS

This book is rooted in the sacred soil of sisterhood. Whenever I pick it up, I shall recall the women who analyzed, argued, questioned, cried, listened, and loved it into concrete form. It would never have been written without the constructive commentary offered by members of my writing group, Mothers Who Write, as well as by participants in my classes and workshops.

As the model took form, Lorena Klinnert, Joy Brown, Denise Schlesinger, and Kathleen Baradaran helped me define the book's message, clarify its target audience, and most important, insisted that I discover, claim, and speak in a voice that was totally my own.

Special thanks to Maureen Walker, a close friend whose sensitive ear for language, alert eye to correctness, familiarity with mythic figures, and regard for me and my story transformed what could have been a tedious task of reading and rewriting into an adventure of inner exploration and personal growth.

I am grateful to the people at Llewellyn Worldwide who transformed my writing into a "real book" and guided it out into the world. My editor, Connie Hill, played a key role in the birthing and naming of this new baby book. Her observant eyes, patient ears, and encouraging heart contributed to an uncomplicated and pleasant period of gestation. Once birthed, *SuperWoman's Rite of Passage* was placed in the care of my publicist, Julie Paxton, and her staff, whom I thank for their past, present, and future efforts. Finally, I want to acknowledge and thank my highly intuitive cover and art designer, Anne Marie Garrison. Her choice of the chambered nautilus not only replicates the Re-Membering model, but also represents a sacred gift of nature that graces my prayer table.

I am especially grateful to my mother, Mary Jacobson, who sustained me through her generous gift of time. By becoming an almost around-the-clock helpmate, she allowed this single mom not only to follow but also to realize a dream. I need to express a love-filled "thank you" to my daughter, Kathryn Scarlett, whose gifts of energy, spontaneity, and honesty brought both light and lightness into even the darkest days and nights.

TABLE OF CONTENTS

"Lazarus, come out!"

John 11:43

PREFACE

Before writing one word of this manuscript, I thought about using the pen name Lazarus. Granted, my body has yet to experience physical death, but my sense of self has died many times during this incarnation and has resurrected from the grave of grief. Part of me died at five, when my father became chronically ill; at eleven, when society's expectations concerning gender-appropriate behavior and roles edited my life's script; at twenty-three, when chemical addiction disrupted our family system; at thirty-seven, when my husband died only four months after the birth of our daughter; at thirty-eight, when my business partner and I experienced a wrenching "parting of the ways," and at forty-two, when the dream of having a second child was shattered in the throes of an abusive relationship. As I reflect upon those "multiple deaths," I see that they share the same cause—loss.

Like many baby girl "boomers," I learned at a young age to live with loss by suppressing negative feelings such as anger, fear, and resentment, disassociating from my own needs and trying to please others. I became competent at and comfortable with stuffing emotions such as anger, fear, shame, and sadness into what I called my "griefcase." That concept came to me during meditation. Upon "seeing" such an object, I realized that I was probably born with an invisible case appended somewhere to my person.

As I grew, so did my griefcase. Because of family rules surrounding the expression of negative feelings, I learned to pack them away with other "dirty linen." The lock on the case was kept secure by denial and silence. The hinges of my griefcase broke following my husband's death after which commenced my rite of Re-Membering.

More specifically, it began quite unconsciously on September 16, 1990. That day, my chronological clock clicked over to forty-five. As my birthday unfolded, I participated in various planned and spontaneous celebrations. Nighttime found me ruminating about several symbols of my success as a Superwoman—a doctorate degree, an enviable resumé, professional recognition, a healthy child in private school, a townhome located in an upwardly mobile neighborhood, and a financial portfolio that gave me a sense of independence.

After adding up the "symbolic spices," in my life, I came to this paradoxical bottom line: I am a successful Superwoman by many standards, but my life still lacks the gifts of self-acceptance and serenity. My stomach did a sudden flip-flop and the two-sided profile of Janus' face flashed across my mind. That image broke my reverie because I knew it represented a deep-seated inner conflict. One side of the face symbolized the "got-it-all-together" mask I wore so comfortably in my role as Superwoman, and the other represented the gnawing feelings of failure and self-doubt. Marti Glenn, a psychologist from Santa Barbara, gave words to what I was feeling that night as I readied myself for bed: "old patterns no longer fit, the new way is not clear, there is darkness everywhere, and she cannot see, feel, taste, or touch. Nothing means much anymore and she no longer knows who she really is."[1]

That night, I had a dream whose variations had recurred over several decades. In it, I am taking pleasure in having put together a larger-than-life puzzle whose pieces, once locked into place, create an image of my face. Just prior to putting the last couple of pieces in place, I notice that a black-booted "someone" enters my space, stands behind my puzzle, and kicks it sharply. Stunned by the blow, I watch my forehead, eyes, nose, and mouth explode out of the frame and land in a pile of disconnected, jagged pieces.

The following morning, I journaled once again about my "booted destroyer." Little did I realize that September 17 marked the day on which I embarked on the longest journey of my life—one that would lead me from my head to my heart, and into the depths of my soul.

After baptizing myself with a splash of cold water, I raised my face from the sink. My eyes caught their reflection in the mirror. Almost magically, the pupils' blackness seemed to envelop me and beckoned me to enter into their three-dimensional space. I stood paralyzed until a series of blinks broke the spell. Sadness rolled over me like a heavy fog. I watched my mouth silently form the words, "Who are you?" Then I screamed that question into the face that gaped back at me. My mask of self-assuredness had broken and, like a toxic chemical, the truth about my Superwoman identity began to seep out. As I stared into the mirror, I felt naked—like a turtle whose protective shell had been stripped away, leaving her softest parts exposed.

A cataclysmic shift in my awareness occurred that morning. It demanded that I begin a myth-making adventure to confront and conquer the booted phantom. I had to answer life's most basic question, "Who am I?"

A few friends and colleagues suggested that I conduct the search for myself on a part-time basis. Others advised me to set those plans aside totally and "get on with my life" through a new career or relationship. In spite of feeling physically exhausted, emotionally frozen, and mentally scorched, I knew mine had to be a full-time, solo quest. In December 1990, I cut the cord that anchored me to the primary source of my Superwoman identity: work. Faith and Courage, my spiritual sidekicks, accompanied me as I took my first step into my midlife rite of Re-Membering.

For months, I felt adrift on a sea of ambiguity. During that time I experienced uncharted realms of my body, mind, heart, and soul. Almost daily, I was plagued with the gnawing thought that I was either going crazy or actively dying. From April through October I was running on "automatic pilot." Memories of those months contain images of returning to bed after dropping off my daughter at school, ignoring dishes and laundry, sobbing uncontrollably at the supermarket, and waking up nightly in the midst of a panic attack. During the bleakest times, I was forced to acknowledge the degree to which my Superwoman's sense of reality had denied the severity of her physical and emotional burnout. I felt relieved by taking a hiatus from work. Only after Superwoman had "hit the wall," did I feel forced to practice self-care by focusing on self-exploration.

For over two years, I worked hard in therapy. I amplified negative memories and feelings in order to understand myself. I actively sought to reconnect with the part of me I had "shelved" in early childhood. In essence, I tried to place my personal and professional history within a spiritual context and to heal the deep gash that had split my identity. Many times I wanted to anesthetize the pain of my self-inflicted agony, but I persevered. In time, I detached from my Superwoman image. I observed her dying and mourned her death. With renewed physical strength, adequate emotional support, and acquired insight into the domains of mythology and nature, I began to heal. I sowed the seeds of my new identity in the ashes of my former self. Hindsight confirmed that I had participated in a death and resurrection event, a rite of passage.

At the outset, I began these pages for myself in order to document my progression toward greater self-knowlege and full personhood. I came to realize that the attainment of such a goal required that I disassemble and reassemble myself. As I participated in my own midlife ritual, I became aware of several middle-aged "Superpeers" who were beginning to disengage from definitions they had formed of themselves. They were questioning their life choices, future options, and familiar identities. After attaining "it all" either at home or at work, why were so many of these "gifted goddesses" feeling burned out, bewildered, and betrayed? Why had Peggy Lee's 1969 hit, "Is That All There Is?" become their theme song? Why were cancerous breasts, diseased hearts, and depressed minds raging as female epidemics? Why was the "bodymind" of millions of suffering sisters crying out in silent rage, "NO MORE!"?

Granted, those questions generate complex answers that are unique to each woman's temperament, social class, natural talents, intelligence, values, family history, and belief system. I discovered a believable response to them, however, in the published works of several feminist authors. Susan Faludi,[2] Emily Hancock,[3] Ruthellen Josselson,[4] Maureen Murdock,[5] Vicki Noble,[6] and Polly Young-Eisendrath and Florence Weidemann[7] explore the idea that in response to patriarchal values, beliefs, and institutions, women, especially high-achieving Superwomen, tend to distance themselves from their innate feminine psyche. As a result, they encounter obstacles that may take an irrevocable toll on their bodies, minds, and spirits.

As I stumbled through my Re-Membering rite, I sensed that a radical shift in self-perception was occurring—not only within me but also within women from diverse racial, political, social, economic, and religious backgrounds. Perhaps the womb of Mother Earth, herself, had begun to contract and to birth a reawakened sense of authority within her disenfranchised, hard-driving daughters. Young-Eisendrath and Weidemann define authority as "the ability to validate one's own conviction of truth, beauty, and goodness in regard to self-concept and self-interest."[8] I began to realize that I had internalized feelings that lacked such authority. My spiritual ear picked up on a silent chant emanating from classrooms, courtrooms, business offices, and bedrooms, as well as across television screens, radio waves, and pages of professional journals, "our time has come … our time has come."

At that point, my reason for writing took on a purpose that reached beyond my personal desire for self-understanding and acceptance. It became important that I reach out to other women who had caught the golden ring of success, only to find it transformed into a self-abusive albatross. During my Re-Membering, I descended into the depths of my own being, crumbled, and died there. I wanted to acknowledge that universal death and rebirth aspect inherent in Re-Membering, to describe the process, and to explore the roles that mythology and nature assumed in my midlife transformation.

During those years of involution and evolution, Mother Nature was my compassionate companion, and mythic goddesses served as mentors. The journey that distanced me from my Superwoman image and brought me back to my feminine source introduced me to Persephone, Demeter, Hestia, Artemis, and Ariadne. It took me almost daily around a lake located close to my home. During those nurturing episodes, Mother Nature spoke to me and revealed "gifts" to me from her domain. Those became ritual objects that I used in my Re-Membering; a forked branch, a feather, a dying tree, a wild rose. Acknowledging my invisible connection to all of those natural wonders, I asked each one to teach me about change, cycles, solitude, and feminine energy. The simplicity of their responses touched me. I decided to weave them into the fabric of my writing.

I hope that I have written *SuperWoman's Rite of Passage* from the perspective of a Re-Membered Adultwoman. What other hopes are interspersed throughout the pages? On a personal level, I hope Re-Membering becomes an objectified symbol that helps me bring closure to my own dance into middle age. Also, I hope that I have provided a different perspective on identity reformation during a pivotal period of a Superwoman's life, and described it with sensitivity, clarity, and candor. I hope that Re-Membering conveys the deep sense of urgency I feel about women's accepting full responsibility for defining themselves, loving themselves, and bestowing their benefic goddess gifts on themselves, families, communities, and planet.

My final hope is that Re-Membering reflects my sacred commitment to spiritual transformation. I hope it enables both men and women to Re-Member their True Selves by loving, honoring, and balancing the tension between the distorted masculine and wounded feminine parts of themselves. May the rite of personal and social Re-Membering deeply affect humanity's conscience by dissolving what Matthew Fox calls the "sin of dualism."[9] My prayer is that such dissolution will create a more bonded sense of community; one that respects affiliation rather than autonomy, encourages cooperation rather than competition, values contextual thought as well as abstract thinking, and resolves conflict through communion rather than confrontation.

During the faltering steps I took at the beginning of my midlife rite of passage, I feared having to do battle with my "booted phantom." Over time, that dreaded demon turned into a dear friend. Through nonresistence, I was able to win the psychic war that pitted my theoretical self against my True Self. Fear, rage, and depression became guides that led me into a Netherworld wherein I found and embraced my feminine soul.

The Greeks gifted us with one of the most wonderful words in English, "enthusiasm." It comes from the words *en theos*, meaning "a god within." Enthusiastically, I bid you success on your transformational midlife journey. Also, I encourage you to share your personal stories, questions, and opinions with me and other sister pilgrims. Abundant blessings, as you begin to fathom the power, wisdom, and sanctity of your Authentic Adultwoman!

Kathleen

There is a void felt these days by women and men—who suspect that their feminine nature, like Persephone, has gone to hell. Wherever there is such a void, such a gap or wound agape, healing must be sought in the blood of the wound itself. It is another of the old alchemical truths that "no solution should be made except in its own blood." So the female void cannot be cured by conjunction with the male, but rather by an internal conjunction, by an integration of its own part, by a remembering or putting back together of the mother-daughter body.

Nor Hall
The Moon and the Virgin

INTRODUCTION

This book is an exploration into the healing realm that Nor Hall describes and recommends. It is the opening of the doors to identity reformation and spiritual growth using mythology, nature, and ritual as keys.

Having opened those doors, a Superwoman, i.e., initiate, crosses an invisible threshold and begins her midlife rite of passage. That event is monumental because, moving from one stage to another, the Synthetic Superwoman faces and moves through the challenge of self-transformation by disassembling and reassembling herself into an Authentic Adultwoman. The Re-membering model embodies many mysteries within its five stages, including death and birth. Goddesses from Greek mythology, as well as objects from Mother Nature's realm are ascribed to each stage to serve as wise and worthy midwives.

The assumption that underlies my book is that, sometime in early childhood, the androgynous or equally gender-balanced psyche of little girls (and little boys, also, for that matter) becomes split and is gravely wounded. As a result of that gash, innately feminine qualities bleed out; that is, they often disappear and are replaced by more masculine qualities that are revered and rewarded within a patriarchal or male-centered culture. Those psychological and social conditions create and foster an environment that produces Synthetic Supermen and Superwomen. At midlife, inner chaos begins to afflict many of those individuals. Sensing a lack of authenticity or reality about their real versus synthetic identity, Superman and Superwoman embark on a journey inward that leads them back to their wounded feminine psyche. By acknowledging and healing that gaping wound, the midlifer rediscovers psychological wholeness and remembers the divine aspect of him/herself, the True Self.

Why have I written only about women, I have been asked. The answer has three parts. The first, very personal, one is that I have been raised in a female body within a male-dominated society. Not unlike other soul-seared sisters, my mind, heart, and spirit were molded during the first half of life, not only to conform to, but also to honor, intellectual, emotional, social, and spiritual norms that frequently conflicted with or demeaned aspects of my innate feminine nature. Because, in the mid-seventies, it appeared far more profitable for high-achieving women to focus monthly on business cycles rather than on moon cycles, I blossomed into what Jacquelyn Small has called a "rolebot"[1] and what I (and millions of others) have called a Superwoman. At midlife, when disassembling and reassembling the synthetic or theoretical self becomes a prerequisite to discovering the True Self, far too many Superwomen are stymied by extreme fatigue, intense frustration, and deep-seated fear. I was terrified! Based upon personal experience as well as anecdotal data drawn from observations of friends, colleagues, and clients, I wanted to reframe a Superwoman's midlife experience by describing it in stages, presenting mentors from mythology, and sharing advice proffered by Mother Nature.

The second reason is just as simple. I see that millions of men are struggling to identify and to use tools that will help them explore the feeling side of their nature—still virginal territory for thousands. I translate the bottom line of that effort to be one of reconciling and bonding with the feminine aspect of themselves. Chanting, drumming, mentoring, marching are all valid means of drawing men into the feminine void. Those activities generate many positive results: improved self-esteem, clearer communication, a broader sense of intimacy, and a stronger relational web that connects them more securely to their True Selves, their parents, partners, children, communities, and God.

The third reason is also quite obvious. I see that our global community is in a critical state. Were we to give a medical prognosis of its status, it might likely be that it is failing to thrive. Such a condition cries out for a different paradigm of human nature and social interaction. Creating and embracing that new model for life on earth will require the wisdom, creativity, compassion, and cooperation of both women and men. Those pathfinders will be neither Superwomen nor Supermen; rather, they will be Re-Membered adults, human beacons of divine light that have been curious and courageous enough to enter and reclaim the feminine void deep within themselves.

The philosophy that underlies Superwoman is the foundation on which all of my work is based. I call the core concept that I teach (and try to live by) *reverential sensing*. It is through the six physical senses (I include mind) that we perceive and judge all people and things in our world. Deep within the center of the feminine void, I envision the existence of a precious jewel, one that allows us to perceive the world reverentially; that is, through spiritual senses. The jewel holds a drop of divine essence that works much like the drop of water in a popcorn kernel. Life celebrations and traumas (births, marriages, deaths, separations, illnesses, addictions) can heat up our physical senses causing us to pop—to think, feel, and behave in certain ways. Re-Membered adults, those who have entered the void and have shed the "Super" image, can pop their spiritual senses out beyond their physical senses. As a result, they perceive their world, even the challenges, with a new-found sense of awe and enlightenment.

When Superwomen embark upon life's midlife rite of passage, they often find that they can enhance their progress by practicing the art of reverential sensing. Within the five stages of the Re-Membering model of transition, Superwoman can expect to experience the mysteries of dying, death, conception, pregnancy, and birth. The themes in *Superwoman's Rite of Passage* underscore those of reverential sensing: the freedom of choice, the unity of all things, the constancy of change, the focus on inner life, the act of letting go, the role of intuition, the need for solitude, and the ultimate gift of self-love.

Superwoman's Rite of Passage is designed to guide readers through a spiritual transition in ways that are personalized, practical, and prayerful. You may choose to use the exercises, rituals, and chapter summaries as self-development tools or as resources for support groups and individual counseling.

Holding a doctorate in education, I market myself as a transformational teacher. As an ex-Superwoman, I now call myself a kitchen contemplative; that is, a modern-day mystic who finds reality hidden more often in the heart than in the mind. To those of you about to embark on an involutionary quest into the feminine void, may these words of Meister Ekhart both motivate and illuminate: "Up then, noble soul! Put on your jumping shoes which are intellect and love, and overleap the worship of your mental powers, overleap your understanding, and spring into the heart of God."[2]

PART I

WHAT IS RE-MEMBERING?

. . . little by little
I came to realize it took
energy to self-remember.

William Patterson
Eating of the I

RE-MEMBERING IS A WORD I came across for the first time while reading a work of Alla Bozarth.[1] So that you and I might share a common understanding of the term, I want to present this definition of it:

> Re-Membering describes a rite of passage that announces a woman's transition into middle age. It unbinds feminine wounds inflicted by beliefs, values, and institutions, and requires the "initiate" or participant to disassemble her familiar definition of self, then to reassemble herself by bringing to mind and honoring her innate feminine "root identity."[2]

To me, Re-Membering is both a process and a product. It identifies what I call a midlife rite of passage. Initially, when I tried to talk about those tumultuous years, I found myself at a loss for words. As a result, I coined one: "terrorific." On one hand, Re-Membering can be a terror-filled time because it makes the participant feel crazy. Painful endings and untidy beginnings generate conflicting behaviors and feelings. They can be scary yet exciting, exhausting yet energizing, fracturing yet healing. On the other hand, Re-Membering can be a "terrific" period in a woman's life in that she begins to focus upon herself, and explore and claim values, interests, and beliefs that belong to her alone. As she Re-Members herself, the midlife "initiate" may think about her life's true purpose. She may actually begin to revise long-held perspectives about herself, others, and even God.

As I began my personal identification quest, I empathized with Hannah Hurnard's allegorical heroine, Much Afraid.[3] Family members and close friends found this admission difficult to accept. I had become powerfully adept at masking my fears. In truth, at midlife, I lacked self-confidence, felt betrothed to Craven Fear, and lived in the Valley of Humiliation. Upon turning forty-five, however, I was compelled to respond to a mandate that came from deep within my being. I had to climb the steep, dangerous mountain of self-transformation—all alone. As I journeyed, I recall the exhilaration that welled inside me when I confronted and communed with unexplored aspects of myself. Re-Membering was a confusing, crazy, but creative time. For me, it embodied the mysteries of death, pregnancy, and rebirth. During that period, I surrendered my familiar image of Synthetic Superwoman, sowed and nurtured seeds of a different identity, then birthed and fell in love with a new sense of me, my Authentic Adultwoman.

Philosophers, theologians, psychologists, and educators have called midlife the threshold into middle age, a crisis, a void, the second adolescence, and the dark night. For me, it was a pivotal time when I was called upon to face the loss of youth, admit failures, and set about recreating my personal mythology.

I had watched some women friends and colleagues dance enthusiastically into the afternoon of their lives and others tip-toe into it, while a few had to be coaxed into acknowledging it at all. I approached midlife reluctantly, experienced it consciously, and emerged from it with a virginal sense of wholeness. In the manner of Emily Hancock,[4] my journey took me through buried memories of childhood. There I had to contact and resurrect aspects of my latent self that I had shelved in early adolescence. That path was painful. Later I followed the dismantling journey of Alice Koller.[5] On it, I met and slew my personal dragons, the familiar but false images I had constructed and accepted of myself. That path was frightening.

RE-MEMBERING AS A PROCESS

At the outset, I need to state that the process of Re-Membering oneself somewhere in the middle of life's stream crosses gender lines. I have elected to describe a female-focused model, however, because midlife carries particularly negative connotations for women, confronts us with myriad transitional events, and represents a time frame during which we begin to discriminate between definitions of "self" imposed by external forces versus those we intuitively know to be valid.

The truth is that I gave a great deal of thought to the process of Re-Membering before I ever wrote a word about it. I read extensively and meditated on the involution and evolution that characterized my life for well over three thousand days. There are some basic assumptions that figure prominently in the process this book describes. I present them here in order to provide a context for the transition model that I sculpted. At the base of the Re-Membering rite is a troubling premise that confronts women growing up in North America. Young-Eisendrath and Weidemann state it this way:

> We are constantly and everywhere subjected to the tacit assumption that males are superior ... Implicitly and explicitly, male norms have become our social standard for physical health, mental health, leadership, relationships, and personal autonom .... women are locked into a double bind in terms of their gender: If they behave as healthy adults they are considered unwomanly, but if they behave as ideal women, they will be considered childlike or inferior .... All women arrive at adulthood with significant feelings of inadequacy.[6]

An Overview of the Model

The Re-Membering model embodies the assumption that North American culture is anthrocentric; that is, it views the world from the perspective of male superiority. I admit that such a viewpoint creates intimidating, painful, and prolonged obstacles for members of both sexes, but I have described my rationale for focusing solely on midlife women. The process of Re-Membering further reflects the assumption that as Synthetic Superwomen develop chronologically and psychologically, they move away from their feminine source of energy and become limited by their own sense of a deficient self. Such "internalized inferiority"[7] undoubtedly contributes to our fears of abandonment, perfectionism, depression, self-hate, as well as other common problems that we often present in therapy. There are two more assumptions that underlie the process of Re-Membering. They are that a woman's identity must be self-engendered, and that contemporary society is on the threshold of a new era, a "Zeitgeist" in which women may redefine their body, mind, and spirit connections by reclaiming an ancient goddess heritage.

Re-Membering, as a rite of passage, focuses on how women refine and reclaim their sense of identity at midlife by leading them back to the roots of their womanly competencies and gifts. It describes a disentanglement process that is characterized by commitment, hard work, and increased internalized growth. Having Re-Membered herself, the initiate is able to experience middle age with a newly-acquired sense of authenticity, autonomy, and authority.

The Re-Membering model reflects a composite of theories that surround human development, change, and grief. I have drawn from materials published in the fields of psychology, thanatology, mythology, spirituality, and adult education. More specifically, the Re-Membering model evolved from works of Mary Catherine Bateson,[8] William Bridges,[9] Elisabeth Kubler-Ross,[10] Carol Gilligan,[11] Jean Baker Miller,[12] Lillian Rubin,[13] and Gail

Sheehy,[14] to cite a few. It describes a five-stage process of identity reformation that marks a woman's transition into middle age.

It would be helpful to think of each of those stages as a step within a spiral pattern, since that form is key to one's movement through the rite. The Greeks called such a pattern the *Dromenon* and considered it holy. It was constructed within temples that honored the Mother Goddess. Alla Bozarth gives us this description of the Dromenon:

> For the Greeks, the Dromenon was a sacred spiral which one followed on foot, in and around and back and in, until one came to the center. At that point, one was healed and renewed in re-membering the Great Mystery and one's place in it .... The Dromenon dance was a turn and return to the matrix of the mother ....[15]

I consciously decided to present the model in the form of a spiral because that pattern represents the choreography a woman must learn and execute in order to complete the Re-Membering dance at midlife (illustrated on page 8). As a mentor from nature, the chambered nautilus reinforces the spiral growth pattern. It shows us how to leave behind outgrown aspects of our lives, forge into new ones, but remain in constant connection to a centralized source of energy and power.

Acknowledging a similar connecting sequence, the Re-Membering model represents a turn and return to a woman's inner core of her identity; that is, her feminine psyche. The stages of the model occur in this order:

Stage I: The Wounds
Stage II: The Dying
Stage III: The Death
Stage IV: The Gestation
Stage V: The Re-Membered Birth

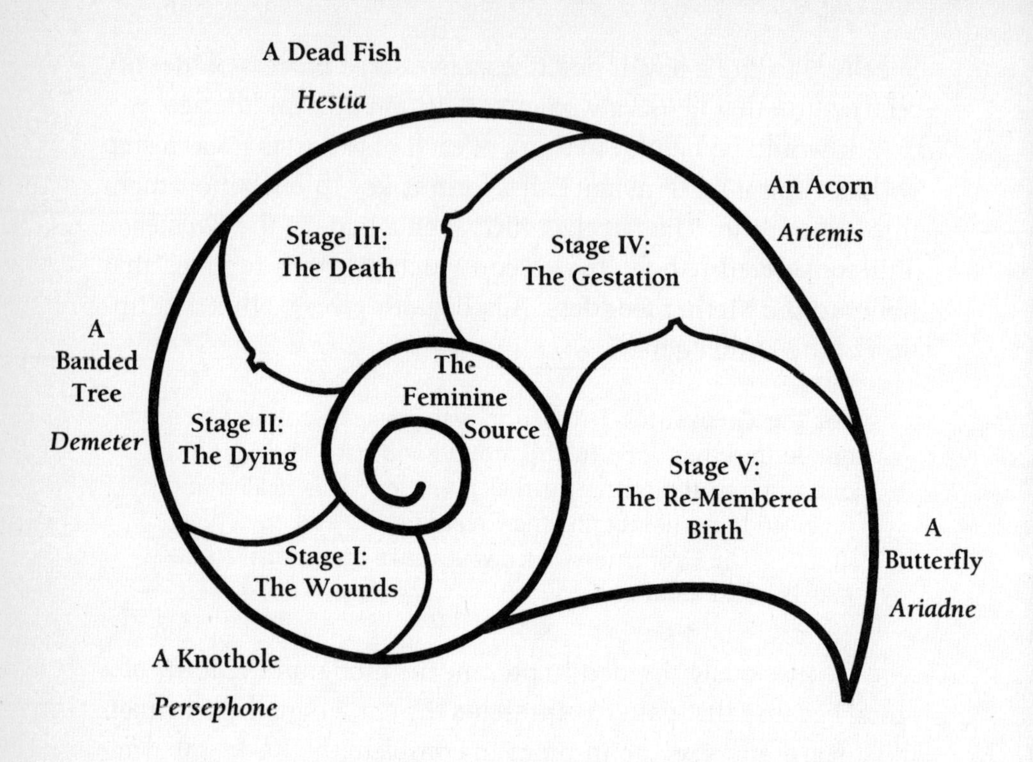

All of the stages relate to the central theme of correcting a woman's often distorted, demeaned, and wounded identity through reunification with her indwelling feminine self. As she masters the task at each stage of the Re-Membering model, the initiate modifies the concept she has both created and acquired of herself.

Each stage within the Re-Membering model presents a task, a symbolic object from nature, and a goddess guide. During my own midlife experience, Mother Nature's voice beckoned to the disowned and dispossessed parts of me. As I walked around the lake or sat by my sacred tree, I found myself watching and listening for teachers to emerge from Mother Nature's realm. I felt caressed by her breezes and comforted with the songs of her bird children. In a similar way, Lesley Shore was nurtured by nature during her midlife quest. She admits "... [Nature] guided me into myself, towards the feminine. She helped me connect with the missing aspects of my self, the lost part. My roots grew into my center, I found fertile ground. I became myself."[16] Finally, Mother Nature offered healing assistance to Much Afraid. On her journey to the Kingdom of Love, Much Afraid collected mementos from nature at each critical juncture. As she stood atop the Mountain of Transfiguration, her Divine Shepherd renamed her Grace and Glory in a ritual that transformed her simple stone treasures into precious jewels.

I discovered that Mother Nature offers her disenfranchised daughters an alternative to the "headucation"[17] we acquire almost hypnotically as we progress through patriarchal institutions of learning and employment. She speaks to us symbolically in a language that consists of her sounds, smells, and ever-changing raiment. As I listened to her with the ear of my heart, I unconsciously began to imitate and to emulate new sounds and novel syntax. Slowly, I began to rewrite my life's script in a language I knew and understood before I ever uttered a word in English.

Although I spent a great deal of time in nature, I also looked to books for insight and affirmation as I Re-Membered myself. I began to read about ancient goddess archetypes. A few became powerful mythic mentors who, for me, held the keys to self-knowledge and wholeness. Jean Shinoda Bolen's work[18] convinced me not only that goddesses reside within every woman, but also that such deities can be invoked for their wisdom and assistance through a woman's innate gift of creativity. I have ascribed a Greek goddess to each stage of the Re-Membering process. My description includes her genealogy and mythology, as well as my rationale for selecting her to represent a particular stage.

Theoretical Assumptions

Having described the model, I want to describe some assumptions that underlie it. You may decide to read these at some later time; however, I feel it important to include them in this chapter.

Stages in the Re-Membering model are cyclic, not linear

This assumption may well be confusing to some readers. Whenever progression through an experience is described in stages, there is a tendency to assume that a person's movement is linear, or in a continuous forward direction. This model acknowledges that, to the contrary, an individual who has progressed to a more advanced stage may intermittently experience feelings and behaviors associated with an earlier stage. Because a woman's movement through the model is cyclic, she may be in Stage IV, gestating a new sense of self, but finds herself at times feeling the pain or experiencing the disbelief associated with Stage l. Such "flashbacks" will be less frequent and less intense than when they were experienced initially, however. It is important that you understand this assumption. Your failure to acknowledge it may result in unrealistic expectations, chronic frustration, or ceasing the process completely.

A woman's definition of self is modified at each stage

My belief is that women in the Re-Membering process must ask themselves the question, "Who am I?" at each stage. Their answers will be different each time because they perceive themselves from a different perspective. In Stages I and II, a woman composes her answer from past experiences, expectations, and environments. It is as if an invisible magnet pulls her awareness backward in the direction of her historic sense of identity. Stage III represents a time during which the initiate may be unable to compose an adequate answer to the question. Indeed, she may turn full-faced into the abyss of her own unknowingness and admit: I don't know who I am. At Stage IV, the magnet pulls her consciousness toward the future. When pondering her identity at this time, the woman begins to explore her wants, identify her needs, respect her competencies, and visualize her dreams. Finally, a Re-Membered human being emerges from Stage V; that is, an Authentic Adultwoman who claims her own identity and finds pleasure and power in it.

Stages within the model are mutually exclusive

It is impractical as well as impossible to draw comparisons between participants who are at different stages in the Re-Membering process. The reason for this is that a woman in Stage I faces tasks, feelings, and behaviors that are different from those facing a woman at a more advanced stage. A woman in Stage I may fantasize about her identity as an Adultwoman; however, she must be willing to give that yet-to-be-realized sense of self-sufficient time to develop.

Progression through the Re-Membering rite is unique to each individual

Neither chronological age nor time have significant impact on a woman's mastery of each task within a stage. Some women may need to spend more time and effort in a given stage, depending upon factors such as honesty, amount of support, physical and emotional strength, unique history, and personality traits.

The Re-Membering rite is a painful event that takes time and commitment

In North America, we are accustomed to anesthetizing pain and to expecting immediate gratification. Tasks within the initial stages of the model may create painful grief reactions. You need to be aware of such outcomes, be willing to experience them, and consider them normal. Sometimes the emotional pain might become so intense that you may consciously elect to cease your movement through the rite. Should that occur, you might reassume the sense of self you had prior to beginning your rite of Re-Membering.

Stage IV, the Gestation, requires time. Our society is an impatient one and feels uncomfortable with uncertainty. During the Re-Membering process, you may often feel enveloped by a cloud of ambiguity. It is disconcerting to reach middle age and to discover that, at some point in your development, you lost touch with your authentic identity—that which remains eternally constant. The desire to fill that void can be compelling. Unless you give yourself sufficient time, you may recreate a false sense of security by falling back on aspects of your former definition of self.

The Re-Membering rite cannot occur in a vacuum

Although a woman moves through the Re-Membering rite alone, the "fallout" from her solo quest imprints and impacts other relationships. First, because your definition of self changes, you may begin to treat yourself differently. For example, you may become more responsible for clarifying your own needs and getting them met. Second, other people who move within your associative web may find it necessary to modify their expectations and behaviors in order to accommodate your evolving identity.

Re-Membering embodies the mysteries of death, conception, and birth

This rite of passage invites the participant to die unto her limited sense of self, then to rise triumphantly, Phoenix-like, out of her own ashes. Like a dying person, you commence your rite of midlife passage feeling a high degree of vulnerability. The emotional pain may become paralyzing as you watch parts of your old self die. Experiencing your own gestation, you seed yourself with authentic interests, values, and beliefs. Finally, you emerge from the rite, once again, virginal with respect to your new identity.

Nature guides women back to the roots of their feminine psyche

I believe that women relate empathically to Mother Nature as "she" executes her cyclic transformations upon the earth and remains intrinsically connected to all forms of life brought forth from her womb. Especially during the Re-Membering rite, it seems fitting that you, the initiate, develop a more intimate relationship with your partners within nature's realm.

Goddess archetypes can serve as mentors to mid-life women

William Patterson tells us "we are all a sea of archetypes."[19] I believe that the Greek goddesses, as mythical images, serve as models to help Superwomen understand themselves better. A woman in midlife transition is faced with surrendering her familiar sense of self and reclaiming an identity from deep within her psyche. You may invoke individual goddesses at each stage of the rite to encourage and assist you in mastering the task associated with each stage in the process.

Re-Membering describes the midlife transition process as experienced by an Anglo, middle-class, well-educated female living in the United States

The observations from which the Re-Membering model evolved are personal. As such, they are limited in terms of their generalizability to broader contexts. While there may be similarities in how women from diverse cultures experience transition at midlife, the Re-Membering model may not represent a process that has universal applicability.

Myths versus Realities

Before I leave this section and begin describing Re-Membering as an educational product, I want to share and to clarify some misconceptions that I had surrounding the process.

MYTH: *I was going crazy.*

REALITY: *I was changing.*

As I questioned and let go of old patterns of thinking about myself and life, everyone and everything appeared to be in a state of extreme flux. Often, it felt as if I progressed two steps forward, then fell five steps back. Such movement created anxiety and frustration in the mind of a woman who had learned to respect and to honor the linear path from point A to point B. Nonlinearity made me feel afraid. Many times, I questioned my sanity.

MYTH: *Re-Membering would be easy—a piece of cake.*

REALITY: *Re-Membering was hard—it hurt.*

Prior to writing this part of the chapter, I reviewed my journal entries and studied some photographs of myself while immersed in the process of becoming an Authentic Adultwoman. Once again, my eyes reflected the silent symphony that played continuously within me. I saw and heard the cacophony of fear, confusion, despair, and rage. At times, the pain became so intense and the fear so overwhelming that I had to anesthetize it. I found I was able to select from a variety of culturally approved strategies, such as spending more time in prayer or at work. Not being above employing nonculturally approved methods of pain control, I went on eating and spending binges. As part of your own rite of passage, you will have to discover the number of ways in which you will try to minimize the duration and intensity of your agony.

MYTH: *Re-Membering would occur quickly.*

REALITY: *With Re-Membering, time became open-ended and out of my control.*

I clearly recall wanting desperately "to get on with my life." I came to despise that feeling and I began to see myself as some kind of insect caught, perhaps forever, on the sticky side of life. Although my theology rejected a punitive place called Limbo, that is exactly where I seemed to be. I had thought that this type of stuckness never happened to card-carrying Superwomen, but it was happening to me. My insistent desire to control the clock and the calendar created resistance to the natural progression of the process. At last, when I assumed the humble posture of nonresistance, I opened up to the rite of passage, and I flowed in harmony with it.

MYTH: *My old self would survive Re-Membering.*

REALITY: *My old self died.*

When I began to Re-Member myself, I envisioned the process as being similar to minor cosmetic surgery. Naively, I thought a change of image might carry me over the threshold, so I cut and colored my hair, then went in for a facial makeover. After several "crazy-making" months, I admitted to myself that Re-Membering required an exploration of self that took me far below epidermal layers. I assumed rather a non-personal attitude as I dissected and discarded parts of my familiar self. The Kathleen whom I had known (and admired) for several decades succumbed during the Re-Membering rite. After I had let go of her, I became pregnant with my new sense of self. That period of gestation seemed to be interminable to me, and to others.

MYTH: *I could Re-Member myself by DOING.*

REALITY: *I Re-Membered myself by BEING.*

This myth was responsible for many false starts before I got serious about commencing my journey. Also, it caused me to accrue hefty bills at book stores, with therapists, and in educational programs. I managed to look for my Re-Membered identity in many wrong places. I believed that if I just read another book, counseled with another professional, or attained another degree, I would find myself and destroy the booted intruder who stalked me in dreams. My roadmap of personal growth had always included doing a variety of tasks. The sacramental act of just being seemed to be sacrilegious to me. In fact, I had no idea of what "just being" really meant. My self-esteem and sense of worth had always been affirmed by achieving something. With simplicity and clarity, Mother Nature illustrated the idea in theory and in practice.

Thus far, I have described the model of Re-Membering and some of the assumptions that underlie it. Because my work represents a guidebook, I want to describe it to you in terms of being an educational product.

RE-MEMBERING AS A PRODUCT

One of the goals I had in writing *SuperWoman's Rite of Passage* is that it serve as a tool for gaining personal insight and facilitate a woman's progression through the midlife rite of passage. I view it as being an educational product or resource. When I taught school, I took special care to present the subject matter interactively to my students and to document my lesson plans in detail. Two-way communication maintained their interest as well as mine, while careful documentation made reference, evaluation, and future planning much easier.

The teacher within me strongly encourages you to journal your progress through the Re-Membering rite. Journaling is a way to document the flow of your life—the endings, in-betweens, and beginnings. I began keeping journals shortly after my husband died. As the years passed, the entries recorded my passionate pursuit of inner growth and personal authenticity. They tapped into my innate gift of creativity and encouraged me to explore the full range of internal and external experiences—from dreams to dragons. Journaling was one way I released feelings, built confidence, and birthed my Authentic Adultwoman.

Because I consider *SuperWoman's Rite of Passage* to be a personal reference manual, I have included "Reflective Exercises" within each chapter. My purpose for doing that is twofold: 1) to encourage your personal participation in the process; and, 2) to document your progression through the rite. I have designed these exercises to be jumping-off points for personal reflection, decision-making, and change. You must remind yourself that pages of a journal contain poignant self-communication from the heart. No one ever need critique your written thoughts or drawings. It is unnecessary to be concerned about your writing style or artistic ability. You need no special talent, training, or timeframe to journal.

I recommend that you complete the reflective exercise segment of each chapter in a quiet place that is conducive to introspection. Also, reserve a block of uninterrupted time to complete the exercises and to journal about them. Deep abdominal breathing, visualization, or listening to music are strategies you might want to employ prior to journaling. After you complete the Reflective Exercise, I suggest that you create and conduct a closing ritual.

Sometimes the word "ritual" conjures up exotic or just plain weird images in a person's mind. Because of its educational intent, *SuperWoman's Rite of Passage* presents concluding rituals for each stage of the process. Kathleen Fischer states: "Ritual is a way in which women can recognize their experiences and name them. Ritual embodies our stories in symbol and action as well as in word and narrative. It also transforms our minds and spirits, and provides meaning for our lives."[20] I view rituals as being powerful vehicles for initiates in the Re-Membering rite of passage to use in bringing closure to past events and in healing wholly into the future.

The rituals that I have suggested are not meant to be prescriptive in nature. There is nothing sacred about them. On the contrary, I see each of them as being a catalyst for expressing your own unique creativity. I strongly encourage you to personalize each one by making it reflect your own needs, wishes, and aesthetic sensitivities.

Each ritual has a specific focus: discernment; purification; surrender; gestation; and celebration. The general template that I have used in designing the Re-Membering rituals is straightforward. My basic suggestion is to create rituals that are both simple and meaningful. You may want to keep these ideas in mind as you bring each stage of the Re-Membering rite to closure:

- Select and prepare a physical space that is comfortable.
- Enhance that space with flowers, pictures, music, etc.
- Incorporate one or more objects to symbolize the four basic elements (air, water, fire, earth).
- Quiet your mind and relax your body before you begin.
- Plan a beginning, middle, and ending.
- Invoke the presence and assistance of the appropriate goddess.
- Do not be afraid to incorporate singing, dancing, or silence.

Now, at last, you are ready to take the first steps of a destiny-making journey. May your heart beat out a steady cadence, your feet execute the complex choreography, your eyes pierce the darkness, and your personal angel guide you inward.

PART II

WHAT ARE THE STAGES OF RE-MEMBERING?

As we grow, we gather new layers,
and as we become well-rounded
in our experiences the layers form
in spiral circles. The layers are
porous ....

Alla Bozarth
At the Foot of the Mountain

As I came to claim the label, Superwoman, I tried to figure out just how I had acquired that synthetic identity. Somewhere along my developmental journey, I had learned to have more respect for the analytical straight line and the concrete than I had for the intuitional spiral and the permeable. Applauding my abilities to attain goals by shooting like an arrow from point A to point B, I embraced the concept of linearity and wove it tightly into the fabric of my life. For decades, I believed that the basic steps in my life's dance consisted of straight lines, deep dips, and sharp turns—similar to those that make up a tango. That outlook may explain the lack of spontaneity and flexibility in my life's choreography as an adolescent. Being rather serious and introverted, I danced across the threshold into young adulthood with my toes to the line, my nose to the grindstone, and my eyes on the prize of "success." By following those leads, I achieved many of the "goodies" that fed a budding Superwoman's soul. Sometime during my mid-thirties, I began to tire of the tango's intense tempo. Instead, I yearned to slow down the rhythm of my life and to waltz gracefully into middle age in three-quarter time. In forging my way through the virginal territories of the Re-Membering rite, I followed a gently curving, spiral path. It took me back into my heart's own inner chamber, wherein I rediscovered the pearl of my True Self.

Though the rite of Re-Membering myself was anything but simple, I find it comparable to the ordinary act of peeling an onion. As I approached Stage I, the paper-thin skin of my Synthetic Superwoman persona had already become brittle. There were times, in fact, when large pieces seemed to crumble away almost eagerly. As I moved through the rite, I began to observe that the layers of my inner self were becoming thicker as a result of suppressed experiences, and juicier because of unresolved feelings. With an invisible scalpel, I started to slice through decades of accumulated myths and misconceptions. Tasks within the first three stages of the Re-Membering model describe aspects of that surgical procedure: acknowledging my wounds; dying unto my former self; and honoring the identity I had sculpted. Unrelated to the mysteries that embody dying, death, and decomposition, the final stages of my Re-Membering rite of passage focused upon the generative acts of conception and birth.

All she knew was that the container she had chosen and found satisfying up to that time, didn't quite fit anymore.

Gail Sheehy
Passages

STAGE ONE: THE WOUNDS

NATURE GUIDE: A KNOTHOLE

One day as I walked around Lake Como, my eyes were drawn to a tree silhouetted near the bank of the lake. I noticed a large, weathered "wound" on its trunk. The knothole captured my curiosity. After staring at it for some time, I tentatively asked, "Do you have something to teach me?"

"I wear this scar with pride," answered the knothole, "for I was wounded in action—carrying out my life's purpose. From your vantage point, it has left me looking unbalanced and unattractive. That perception is an illusion. Because of this wound, I have discovered inner wisdom and power. It serves me as another eye whose focus is inward. Because of its gift of inner vision, I have been able to acknowledge and to embrace most losses in my life. Can you make that claim for yourself?

"Loss is one of those words that citizens of your kingdom seldom want to acknowledge. There is a good chance that it will stir up feelings of pain and fear. As a result, your people start to close their eyes to loss while still very young. Even the tenderest of shoots is not immune to loss. Like their adult counterparts, children experience loss through their normal development, close attachments, and bitter betrayals. There still lives within you that tender shoot of yourself, the eternal child. What physical or emotional losses are part of that little one's history? Did she, like me, experience any amputations? It is essential that you call her out from the recesses of your mind. She holds the light to inner illumination.

"Loss is one way that Mother Nature offers her children the gift of growth. Naturally, our acceptance of loss involves choice. Choose to become a conscious loser. By following that strategy, you will become a conscious winner at the game of life. Identify your wounds, especially those inflicted in the experience known as childhood. Use your imagination to enter and to explore each one. Invite your eternal child within to accompany you to this Never Never Land of your own making. She will be the instrument of grace that brings you total trust, steadfast courage, and ultimate victory on your quest. Play make-believe with her and give your wounds permission to talk to you. Through them, you will rediscover the ancient mandate to love yourself."

For some time, I gazed at that weathered cyclopian hole. With my perception expanded, I no longer viewed it as disfiguring, but rather as a mark of beauty. I began to wonder what had happened to the limb. Had it become the victim of a daring child's afternoon adventure? Did it crack under the strains of winter's prolonged wrath? I realized that, like the knothole, each of my life's scars claimed a history. For too long, I had denied and even damned their existence.

Suddenly, I needed to see my scars. I wanted to name each wound and touch it. With closed eyes, that thought created an image in my mind. I envisioned my body and noticed several indelible scars marking loss events. Time identified older ones with shiny flesh. More recent scars glowed with a subtle kind of rawness. A few other wounds had healed over, but looked infected. Those begged to be incised and drained of unresolved emotional matter. The thought of re-opening emotionally-infected lesions felt scary, but somehow timely.

Next, I imagined all of my losses marked off chronologically on a line. I was surprised by the events that generated some of the scars because they seemed insignificant at the time they were inflicted. Perusing my loss-line, I was struck by its multi-dimensional nature; there were physical, mental, emotional, and spiritual losses. While I was able to classify them into those specific domains, the impact of each loss created "fallout" that failed to respect defined boundaries. For example, emotional scars affected my body as well as my spirit. My attention, then, was drawn to my stomach. There, I was reacting to the wounds with mixed feelings of pride, sadness, anger, and fear. That response left me with a sense of profound confusion surrounding my own scars. One part of me pleaded to cease this self-examination, another urged me to persist.

Contemporary life in North America allows little time to acknowledge or to reflect upon loss. As children, we are not taught ways of either identifying or coping with everyday losses and the changes they generate. On the contrary, some of the events for which youngsters grieve are ignored or minimized by people around them. In not-so-subtle ways, the word "loss" has acquired some lexical connotations similar to other four-letter words that are best left unspoken. No one wants to lose, be a loser, or be for a loser. On the contrary, we are encouraged to look out for and be "Number One."

My wounded wisdom teacher had advised me to become reacquainted with the eternal child that dwelled somewhere within my psyche. Having closed my eyes, I breathed myself back in time. Slowly, pictures began to bubble up to the surface. I saw long blond curls, a doggie blanket, a tricycle, and bib overalls. "Cookie" responded to my silent call, and she had something to say. Intent on holding her image in mind, I picked up my journal and sketched her. She was sitting on a hillside and was surrounded by flowers. I knew they were jonquils and each one wore a happy face. Cookie's countenance, on the other hand, was sad. Her eyes were closed, and tears ran down her cheeks. With arms wrapped tightly around her knees, she began to rock and to talk. Below is an excerpt from my journal entry of May 2, 1991.

> Cookie: "Everything's got a happy face around here but me. I'm sad 'cause you were always too busy to be with me. Now, I'm not going to look at you 'cause you never looked at me. I've been mad at you for a real long time. I've even wanted to kick or to bite you so you'd look at me."
>
> Me: "I can see that you are sad and hear that you are mad at me. It still feels so good to be with you now, Cookie. I really wanted to spend more time with you, but all of a sudden, it felt as if I had to grow up. I thought I had to stop playing with you after my father got sick. I was tired a lot of the time and I felt scared because of all the pain and uncertainty. I couldn't be with you because I had to help my mom make everything feel OK at home. I'm sorry."
>
> Cookie: "You lost out on a whole lot by not being with me more. Sad thing is that I was a big loser, too."
>
> Me: "What exactly did I lose, Cookie?"
>
> Cookie: "You lost me when you left behind my world of fantasy and magic. You lost what you call childhood. Deep down I'm real happy that you've come back for me. I still want to be your best friend. I'll keep holding your hand if you just promise to do three things: hear me, see me, and play with me once in awhile."

I felt myself being buried by an emotional avalanche of pain and sadness. Holding the journal close to my heart, I began singing the following words to the melody of a well-known Catholic hymn, "Immaculate Mary."

Cookie's Song

Cookie I love you, I'm so glad I found you
For years you've been hidden away in my heart
I love you, want you, need you, respect you
You are my treasure, you are my joy.

Before continuing my walk that day, I thanked my humble teacher, the knothole, for imparting its single-eyed sense of vision to me. I left that spot knowing that a) loss, like air, is a natural, essential aspect of life; b) like beauty, it lies in the eye of the beholder; and c) like a wound, it heals, in time, but may leave a scar, "where once an open wound burned unbearably, now a thin transparent scar."[1]

I sang "Cookie's Song" hundreds of times during my Re-Membering. She assumed the roles of both playmate and guide throughout my transformational rite of passage. Often I would find her woven into the fabric of my unconsciousness. Especially during Stages I and II, this dream would recur with few variations.

I would find myself in one of the rooms of my parents' home. Based on my physical appearance, I ranged in age somewhere between early adolescence and mid-teens. Consistently, I would be pregnant. I never experienced the negative feelings of fear, shame, or anger about the pregnancy. On the contrary, it gave me great joy. All alone in our bathroom, I would give birth to a healthy, full-term daughter. Hugs and kisses expressed the deep love that I felt for my little girl. Shortly after her birth, I would walk into my bedroom. There, I would pick up a doll whose front half snapped into the back half of its body. Methodically, I would open the doll, lay my live baby in the doll-like sarcophagus, cover her with the front half of the toy, then snap the two parts together. Finally, I would lift the doll up and hold her directly in front of me. Her closed eyelids would slowly open, but there would never be eyes in the sockets. That dream spoke to me of my lost childhood, my lost Cookie. Her gifts of childlike trust, spontaneity and honesty were to become the stars that illumined the blackness of some of my soul's darkest nights.

The Goddess Guide: Persephone

What is Persephone's genealogy?

The Greeks called her Persephone and the Romans evoked her as Proserpina or Cora. While Persephone was not among the first generation of Olympians, she was born of the clandestine union between Demeter, the earth-goddess, and Zeus, the sun-god and her sibling. According to Jean Shinoda Bolen, "Greek mythology is unusually silent about the circumstances of her conception."[2]

In Hellenic times, Persephone was worshipped in two distinct ways, as the Kore or fertile young Maiden, and as the mature Queen of the Underworld. According to Kerenyi, Persephone "acquired the name, 'the maiden,' when, as first and only daughter of her mother, she fell victim to the god of death (Hades, brother of Zeus)."[3]

As Queen of the Underworld, the goddess ruled over the dead and guided both mortal and immortal visitors to and from her subterranean realm. Persephone and her mother became central figures in the Eleusian Mysteries, a major religion of Greek men, women, children, and slaves. The purification, sacrificial, and other ceremonial rites of those mysteries were transmitted orally by priests who, like all initiates, were bound by secrecy. Morford and Lenardon conclude: "It seemed fairly certain that one major common denominator (of the Mysteries of Eleusis) is the belief in man's immortal soul and future life."[4] Bolen states: "In the Eleusian Mysteries, the Greeks experienced the return or renewal of life after death through Persephone's annual return from the Underworld."[5] Some of the less profound secrets and rituals of the Eleusinian rites are revealed in the Homeric Hymn to Demeter. It is there, too, that Persephone is described, along with her relationship to Demeter and abduction to the Underworld by Hades.

What is Persephone's mythology?

As Demeter's only child, Persephone was raised on Olympus. The major myth associated with this goddess describes her abduction into the world of the Underworld by her uncle, Hades.

While playing one spring day, Persephone catches sight of an unusual, fragrant narcissus plant. As she reaches out to touch a bloom, the earth opens and Hades emerges from the depths in his chariot drawn by several black steeds. He snatches up Persephone and they disappear into the realm of the dead.

Demeter becomes inconsolable with grief and rage. She leaves Olympus, taken up residence in the home of Kelios, King of Eleusis, and caused all of earth's bounty to wither. A terrible famine has stalked the land, and humans have stopped offering gifts and sacrifices to the gods. Through various gods and goddesses, Zeus implores Demeter to allow the earth to bring forth its bounty. Demeter agrees to honor Zeus' request only if she is able to see Persephone once again. Zeus accepts the goddess' compromise, asking Hermes to communicate the decision to Hades.

While in the dark realm of the Underworld, Persephone remains overwhelmed by acute grief. She is unwilling to partake of the food of the dead (the pomegranate), and longs for the companionship and love of her mother.

Hermes finds Hades sitting alone with Persephone. He explains his reason for traveling across the River Styx. Upon hearing this, Persephone leaps for joy, and Hades defers to the will of his brother. Before allowing Persephone to accompany Hermes out of the realm of the dead, Hades surreptitiously places three pomegranate seeds in her mouth, assuring her cyclical return for a third of each year to the Underworld as his Queen.

When Persephone finds her mother in the temple built for her at Eleusis, Demeter is overjoyed. She then causes the earth to give forth its bounty once again, and both mother and daughter remain in together, teaching the sacred rites and rituals that have come to be known as the Eleusisisn mysteries.

What makes Persephone a mythic mentor?

I have selected Persephone, "the goddess of the budding shoots,"[7] to guide midlife maids and matrons through the first stage of the Re-Membering rite of passage. My intent is to underscore the fact that, despite their chronological age, women at this stage are about to enter a virginal realm within themselves. To make that journey, they will need to a) acknowledge the wounds inflicted upon their feminine psyche as a result of their abduction into a patriarchal culture; b) question and surrender their naive trust of institutions and people from whom they have constructed their sense of identity; and c) experience conflicted feelings, such as love/hate or trust/betrayal, as they contemplate the dismemberment of the image they have created of themselves.

In *Goddesses in Everywoman,* Persephone is classified as one of the three vulnerable goddesses; those abducted, raped, dominated or humiliated by male gods. Like Demeter and Hera, Persephone was "relationship-oriented ... whose identity and well-being depended on having a significant relationship ... [she] suffered when attachment was broken or dishonored."[8]

My rationale for selecting Persephone as a guide to initiates at Stage I is that she represents a duality inherent in women—the Kore or "nameless maiden who does not know who she is and is yet unaware of her desires and strengths,"[9] and the Queen of the Underworld who "moves back and forth between the ego-based reality of the 'real' world to a place where memories and feelings have been buried."[10] Many Superwomen approaching midlife sense that they lack an authentic identity and fail to appreciate the feminine gifts of wisdom, creativity, intuition, and spirituality that lie deep within themselves.

There are additional reasons for selecting Persephone as a mentor to women commencing their transition at midlife. First, Persephone as Kore embodies the passive, compliant woman. As Queen of the Underworld, she matures through self-knowledge and acceptance, then "claims for herself what she wants."[11]

Second, like this mentor, many middle-aged women have devalued or severed their connection to their feminine competencies and gifts in order to survive in a male-dominated culture. Third, while in Hades, Persephone found herself in a nonnurturing environment and failed to nurture herself. Often, contemporary women must function in work and home environments that become abusive. Like Persephone, they withdraw into a depressed state and may expend even more emotional and physical energy attempting to make their circumstances and themselves more perfect and more successful. Fourth, Persephone had to journey into the darkest recesses of herself to realize her full personhood. There, she confronted and claimed her sexuality, spirituality, and independence. Fifth, like Persephone, initiates at Stage I struggle between intense feelings of wanting to remain attached to their assumed identity and needing to separate from it. Finally, as Queen of the Underworld, Persephone agreed to a compromise that gave her the power and permission to move freely between her inner, feminine-centered life, and the outer, male-oriented world.

What are some of Persephone's qualities?

Persephone exhibits certain traits that are needed by the Stage I initiate. The abduction myth introduces Persephone at play with her girlfriends. In that female-centered environment, Persephone's behavior is that of a spontaneous, curious spirit intent on being receptive to and trusting of all life brings her. In fact, she reaches out confidently to pluck the narcissus, the most beautiful flower in the meadow.

Emily Hancock suggests that, around the age of nine, the self-confident Persephone-type maiden yields herself to self-consciousness by "donning the masks provided by the culture and losing sight of who and what she is beneath the feminine façade she adopts."[12] In Hancock's opinion, "rediscovering the girl within [the Kore] appears to be the key to woman's identity."[13] To take the first steps of her midlife ritual dance, the initiate must evoke her indwelling Kore and draw upon the self-reliant and self-directed maiden she was prior to "falling victim to the depressing shadow of success."[14] The initiate must commit to claiming her own authenticity by reaching for the blossom whose shoots are rooted deep within her own heart.

Persephone's strengths are numerous; for example, her optimism, confidence, spontaneity, curiosity, receptivity, and willingness to assume risk. The initiate at Stage I needs those qualities in order to master the goals associated with this stage. There are some traits of both Maiden and Queen, however, that can impede a participant's progress.

Persephone was engaged in a lifelong dependent relationship with her mother. Undoubtedly, the degree of their bonding was significant in creating her diffused or unclear sense of identity. She might not have known where Persephone began and Demeter ended. Frequently, contemporary women are challenged by boundary issues surrounding their biological mothers and other significant relationships. Because of women's tendency to define themselves through affiliations, boundaries can be especially complex. The conflict between being selfish versus selfless often becomes a compelling one.

After her initial protestations, Persephone exhibited a sense of powerlessness following her abduction by Hades. She seemed to accept her victimization compliantly, but fell into a silent, chronic depression. Like her mythic mentor, the Stage I initiate may feel that, as captive to and victim of patriarchal constructs, she lacks control over the dictates imposed by them. As a result, she may become depressed, a symptom that could conceal repressed anger or even rage.

Persephone, the Kore, displayed an innocent naivete that was dispelled after her abduction to and sojourn in the Underworld. At the onset of midlife, the Kore initiate may exhibit similar attitudes toward youthfulness and perfection. She may reach out through a variety of means, ranging from low-impact aerobics to cosmetic surgery, to maintain her youthful demeanor. Her desire to deny middle age and to pluck eternal perfection from within and outside of herself could become frustrating and confusing. Young-Eisendrath and Widemann describe the Catch-22 condition in which the Kore woman may find herself: "... women are locked into a double bind in terms of their gender; if they behave as healthy adults, they are considered unwomanly, but if they behave as ideal women, they will be considered childlike or inferior."[15]

Stage I Tasks and Strategies

Stage I of the Re-Membering rite of passage embodies the broad goal of identifying past wounds, especially those that have pulled Superwoman away from her feminine core.

There are several strategies you might choose to employ during this stage of your transition process. I have described a few of them below:

- ✧ Develop keen skills of self-observance in order to validate the reality of past and present losses. Invite your "observer self" to draw its life-line from birth to the present. Identify each loss event and note its date on the timeline. Peruse the list and identify any wounds that remain unhealed.
- ✧ Assess your personal strengths and vulnerabilities honestly as a means of increasing self-esteem. List ten competencies that you claim personally, socially, or professionally. List ten aspects of your personal, interpersonal, or professional self that render you vulnerable.
- ✧ Commit to the Re-Membering process in order for personal growth to occur and authentic identity to emerge. Communicate your intent to someone else (a friend, colleague, or counselor) who will listen to and affirm your progress, yet hold you accountable to your commitment.

- Engage in activities that call forth your feminine gifts of intuition, creativity, psychic abilities, and healing.
- Read about those topics or attend seminars on them. Maintain a personal journal, especially concerning your dreams.
- Create an inventory that profiles and distinguishes between your goals, interests, values, and beliefs and those imposed by culturally-based gender expectations. Print resources such as *The Creative Journal*[16] and *The Inventurers*[17] may prove especially helpful.
- Develop insight into the impact of a patriarchal society on female psychosocial development. Read published material or attend workshops on topics related to female development, female spirituality, and goddess mythology. Some suggested titles include *The Heroine's Journey*,[18] *In A Different Voice*,[19] *The Feminine Face of God*,[20] and *The Goddess Re-Awakening*.[21]
- Talk to someone about who you are, as well as how you feel about mid-life transition, middle age, and growing up in a male-dominated culture.
- Cultivate a network that provides educational and/or emotional support. Possible resources could include churches, synagogues, business and professional organizations, advocacy groups, and counseling centers.
- Schedule time for self-nurturance and fun.

Stage I's Major Obstacle

Listen carefully to messages you may be sending yourself either consciously or unconsciously. Do any of these sound familiar?

> Someone or something will rescue me from this situation.
>
> I can do and have it all.

Like mother, like daughter.

I'm not growing older, I'm growing better.

Time will take care of this problem.

I can't buck the system.

In her wisdom, Alla Bozarth observes, "a defective starter button is the greatest deterrence to any artist...."[22] Denial is an endemic deterrent for women either beginning the Re-Membering process or moving from Stage I to Stage II. It is a self-destructive habit that is learned at an early age and reinforced as a young girl develops. At midlife, old patterns and attitudes send push-pull messages between who women think they are, who they really are, and who they hope to become. According to Freudenberger and North, "Since most (women) were raised with enforced gender limitations that 'goodness of fit' (unity between what is wanted and what is needed) may feel awkward and out of sync with the needs of the True Self."[23] They go on to assert that "many women have become so inured to inequities and injustices in order to survive, they may have learned to 'go dead' in order to survive."[24]

The primary task facing the initiate at Stage I is to identify and to own her wounds. That action is bound to create unpleasant feelings and to generate pain. Enterprising and experienced Superwomen have learned sophisticated techniques to deny their scars. Some may consciously suppress information that is painful or stress-producing. A more subtle strategy is to cover it up with a joke about their fatigue, fear, anger, or unequal status. Frequently, women rationalize the existence of their wounds by labeling themselves in ways that are denigrating. For example, they may defend their behavior and define themselves by saying, "I'm codependent, I'm a caretaker, I'm a late bloomer, or I've always been unsure of myself."

Finally, because of the multitude of roles and responsibilities she assumes, a contemporary Superwoman may stay busy or get even busier in order to avoid having to let go of myths she has woven around her identity. An unconscious devotion to denial may stymie a woman's movement toward resurrecting her authentic self. Denial acts as a catalyst for feeling and for acting "stuck."

A Reflective Exercise

Find a comfortable space where you can relax and reflect upon these questions. When it is suggested that you sketch part of your answer, please do so. It will help you tap into conscious and unconscious feelings that surround your loss. You may choose to complete this exercise in a Re-Membering journal.

a) Write down the word, LOSS. Look at it for some time. What images and feelings does the word evoke in you?

b) Look over the losses that appear below. Check all of the "wounds" you have experienced. List others you know personally that are not included in the list.

☐ Death of parent, spouse, sibling, child, grandparent	☐ Chronic mental illness
	☐ Chronic physical illness
☐ Divorce	☐ Surgery
☐ Separation	☐ Menopause
☐ "Empty Nest"	☐ Infertility
☐ Retirement	☐ Miscarriage
☐ Unemployment	☐ Abortion
☐ Unrealized dreams (future, child, career, mate)	☐ Loss of possessions (home, car, money ...)
☐ Other:	

c) Do any of the losses from your list still "feel" unhealed? Which are they? Where do you feel them in your body? What do you think prevents healing from occurring? How might you facilitate such healing?

d) Sketch the first major loss you can recall. What happened? How old were you? How were you told of the loss? How did you respond? What support, if any, did you receive?

e) Think about the most significant loss in your life. Draw the scar from that wound. Invite the wound to talk to you. What does it say? What positive outcomes, if any, have resulted from that loss?

Ritual for Stage I: Transforming Old Wounds

The gift that comes to you through this ritual is that of discernment; that is, the identification of past personal losses. Remember, it is important that you be able to claim ownership of your closing ritual. Read over the one that appears below. Feel free to pick and choose parts of it that feel right to you. Also, take this opportunity to honor your own gift of creativity. A seed thought is an idea that you want to carry consciously into your closing ritual. Take a moment to read the thought for Stage I, either silently or aloud.

SEED THOUGHT:

I need not look upon my wounds as stumbling blocks, but rather as stars that illumine my chosen path to wholeness.

Should you choose to complete this ritual step-by step, here are some materials you will want to place on your "altar": a candle, a live plant, a photograph of yourself around the age of nine or ten, a glass of water, slips of paper and a pencil, a shallow dish or ashtray, and matches.

In a space you find comforting (consider lighting, temperature, furniture, etc.), prepare your body, mind, and heart for what is about to unfold.

Light the candle and gaze at your photo. Claim this truth: "I who was still am." Close your eyes and allow the memory of the candle's flame to guide you inward.

Connect with your breath. That will center you and allow you to claim your human inheritance of life and death with each inhalation and exhalation. You might want to do this eight to ten times.

Hold the plant and invoke the presence and help of Persephone, your indwelling "goddess of the budding shoots." Through your imagination, experience her in your presence. Some invocations you may choose to use appear below:

Invocations

Persephone, help me to be open and receptive.

Persephone, teach me to honor my wounds.

Persephone, keep me committed to Re-Membering.

Persephone, guide me between my inner and outer worlds.

Persephone, strengthen me to separate from familiar attachments.

Bring to mind the different types of losses (wounds) that you have experienced. Using your small slips of paper, jot down each one that you would like to let go of as part of this ritual. Have you identified any that you are still grieving? Have you written down anything that surprises you? Remember, your eternal child may have experienced losses that you have minimized or overlooked. After you have named your wounds, place them in the ashtray or bowl. Realize that letting go of your wounds in the context of this ritual will not automatically result in eliminating them from your mind or heart. Long-term forgiveness or reconciliation may require healing over time.

Pick up the dish that contains your "wounds." Give thanks for them, then set fire to them. As you watch them burn, claim this thought: *Out of the ashes of past wounds, I, like the Phoenix, shall rise Re-Membered.* When all of the wounds have been burned, pour some water on them as a symbol of cleansing and completion.

Take a few moments to sit in silence. Be aware of any images and thoughts that cross your mind.

Close your ritual with a prayer, reading, or music of your choice.

SUMMARY

STAGE I: THE WOUNDS

NATURE GUIDE
A Knothole

MYTHIC MENTOR
Persephone

MENTOR QUALITIES
Virginal
Maiden/Maid duality
Female-centered environment
Spontaneous
Curious
Trusting
Risk-taking
Experienced in the Underworld

PRIMARY TASK
To identify wounds from the past.

PRIMARY STRATEGIES
Become self-observant
Assess personal strengths
Network with peers
Commit to the process
Nurture yourself

MAJOR OBSTACLE(S)
Denial

RITUAL FOCUS
Discernment

WHOM MIGHT YOU ENCOUNTER?
Your Eternal Child

Part of me is dying
maybe to let the the rest
of me come to life.

Stephen Levine
Meetings at the Edge

STAGE TWO: THE DYING

NATURE GUIDE: A DYING ELM

Late one August afternoon, I sat in my sacred spot watching the clouds roll across the sky. I hoped to hear Mother Nature's voice whispering, but knew that she unveiled her inspiration without much ado or fanfare. I just closed my eyes and waited.

When at last I opened them, I noticed that the trees along the shoreline had extended long, finger-like shadows. The most surrealistic of them was created by an elm just off to my left. Earlier, the enormous trunk and canopy had failed to capture my attention. That day, my glance was fixed upon a wide band of red paint that encircled its trunk. I knew it meant the tree was diseased and had to be cut down. Respectfully, I acknowledged my Nature Guide: "What have you to teach me?" my heart asked.

"Don't stare! We're both terminal. My death band is similar to the invisible one you wear. It represents the cosmic union that indwells all living things—the marriage of life and death. Over time, I have grown comfortable wearing this blood-red band.

"At first, I despised it. I hoped that heavy rain would wash it away, but death's fingerprint proved to be indelible. It announced my eminent death in a way that seemed brash. I felt embarrassed.

Also, I resented the trees around me that had escaped the banding brush. For some time, I struggled with the question, 'Why me?' until it began to strangle me. Finally, I saw myself as betrayed by Mother Earth, whose womb had nurtured and whose nutrients had sustained me over decades.

"In time, I was able to accept my fate. At that point, I decided to die consciously. Doing that meant I had to reach well beyond the tips of my branches. I had to wrestle with some perplexing questions: Where were my roots? What were my anchors? What was really dying inside me? How was I honestly feeling?

"My decision to die consciously has given me permission to leave home; that is, to move away mentally from the familiar, comfortable, and accepted truths I once embraced. I have moved beyond former edges of self-awareness by shearing away deeply conditioned images and beliefs.

"Right now, your True Self and your theoretical self are engaged actively in battle. As a result, some fraudulent parts of your public image will be exposed and will become war casualties. Be merciful with yourself and mourn. As one surrenders to unknown aspects of this divinely ordinary event called dying, seeds of a new and more authentic life will germinate, and become anchored to the Authentic Adultwoman you are to become."

When I reread the thoughts shared with me by my Guide, my feelings were ambivalent; reassured yet anxious. I was relieved at talking so openly and personally about dying.

My banded teacher had spoken wisely. Indeed, all living things are wedded inextricably to their eventual death. Within North American culture, however, dying remains a much unexplored frontier. Our first tendency is to deny it, then we tend to prolong life with all our technological, emotional, and spiritual know-how.

The fact that a battle was raging within me came as no surprise. Evidence of such a fray had surfaced simultaneously in my personal and professional life, as well as in my inner world of dreams. The thought of not only exposing fraudulent parts of myself but also allowing them to die produced feelings of deep shame and of paralyzing fear.

Like the elm, I viewed those parts of my identity as being imperfections or chinks in my Superwoman's armor. They were embarrassments. As I observed many female friends and colleagues, I grew envious and resentful of their continued ability to have and do it all. The thought that my hard-earned self-image was dying scared me. At times, I felt so afraid that I threw up, then wondered if, on a literal level, my body was trying to expel some kind of poison. Finally, I, too, felt betrayed by matriarchal forebears. How had they become invisible? When had their talents and gifts become debased? Why had their voices remained silent? At this moment, might the cosmos be kissing the ancient goddess into an awakened state? That thought made me feel excited.

Another idea that I received from my Guide concerned leaving home; emancipating myself from long-held expectations of who I should be and what I should be doing. Anderson and Hopkins describe how home-leaving happens for many women: "... some hidden timing stirs us. We wake up one morning to find we are no longer able to squeeze into our old identity. What used to feel secure and comfortable now feels life-denying."[1] Ever so slowly, I came to view the act of dying as being life-affirming. I had created and sustained my Synthetic Superwoman image of myself at unknown costs to my body, heart, mind, and soul. In permitting those reflections to die, I was willing my Authentic Adultwoman to live. As I sat next to my Guide, I realized that I was on the threshold of a doorway that opened onto untold entitlements. I was committed to walking through death's door, even if my steps were halting and baby-sized.

In the footsteps of my Nature Guide, I wanted to die consciously. That meant that I had to face deep-seated fears and struggle with complex questions. Where, for example, were the roots of my identity? With hard work and professional help, I discovered that, for decades, my root system had been growing in a horizontal direction. In fact, it appeared to thrive in a rich, but thin, top-soil composed of patriarchal attitudes, unresolved grief, and an indefatigable need to achieve, to be perfect, and to succeed in a man's world. As I approached midlife, my root system began to grow vertically; that is, inward. At that point, some of the roots withered and others died in the search for more fertile soil. It was then that I began to perceive my symbolic dying as being a preparatory step to replanting. I knew that my new root system would grow deep into the source of my feminine psyche.

Another question raised by my Guide concerned anchors. Specifically, what were mine? Ruthellen Josselson relates anchoring to identity formation in women. She states that "... (anchoring) is a way of attaching to aspects of the adult world, of having a berth in it."[2] Prior to this stage of my life's journey, my anchor points were located outside myself. They related to members of my original family, my daughter, my academic accomplishments, and my entrepreneurial endeavors. There was no anchor that hooked me securely to my True or Authentic Self. Only after objectively assessing the internal and external aspects of my anchors was I able to address the midlife tasks of standing alone, setting individual goals, and claiming my authenticity. With childlike faith, I came to believe in the transformative power of these words: "I am my own anchor."

At some point in Stage II, I became able to admit that some roots within me were dying and others were in need of re-anchoring. What, though, was actually dying? After meditating a long time on the question, I came to understand that three Great Pretenders, creations of my theoretical self, were actively dying. Those were images of myself as "Helpless Victim," "Perfect

Mother," and "Masterful Male." Those roles or subpersonalities had begun to resemble over-sized balloons with pin-point leaks. Without constant maintenance, they became flaccid and useless. Because I had learned to relate to them as friend, confidante, and even lover, it was painful to deny them life support, and worse yet, to witness their death. Through the painful grace of discernment, I chose to tear myself open, expose those parts of my public persona that were dying, and forgive myself for having become overly dependent upon them.

While I was dying unto myself, my feelings ran the gamut of grief's reactions. Perhaps my most constant companion was fear. I was scared that upon the death of manufactured masks nothing of real worth or substance would remain. I also felt outrage at society's blatant endorsement of a patriarchal perspective. It had sold me "a bill of goods," and I was angry with myself for having bought into its seductive packaging. In total candor, there were times when I felt immobilized by sadness. I became severely depressed. During such episodes, I pined for my Great Pretenders and yearned to resurrect them. The longer I lived out my own death-watch, however, the more my urge to leave home grew stronger, my resistance to letting go grew weaker, and my dream of wholeness became clearer. Somehow, the negative emotions that surrounded my dying became balanced by positive feelings of joy, peace, and love. I experienced those when I thought of mothering myself. I trusted that my now-empty womb would eventually receive and nurture new life—my Authentic Adultwoman.

The Goddess Guide: Demeter

What is Demeter's genealogy?

The Greeks called her Demeter, while the Romans worshipped her as Ceres, from which name the word "cereal" is derived. She was one of the major Olympian goddesses, the mother of Persephone, the mother of grain and harvest. Some etymologists think that part of Demeter's name means "mother." That identity is tightly woven into the maternal tapestry that Demeter dons in her roles of the Generous Mother, the Grieving Mother, and the Destructive Mother.[3]

Demeter was the second child of seven born to Kronos and Rhea. Sadly, at the birth of each child, Kronos would swallow the infant whole. He feared that his progeny would overthrow him as he had overthrown his father. Rhea was able to hide one of her sons, Zeus. Instead of handing the child to Kronos, she wrapped a stone in infant's clothing. The child was reared in secret and grew up to marry Metis, a Titan woman who gave Kronos an emetic. He proceeded to vomit forth all of his children. Zeus and his siblings overthrew their father. Zeus then became consort to his sister, Demeter, and they begot the maiden goddess, Persephone.

What is Demeter's mythology?

The Homeric "Hymn to Demeter" relates the abduction of Persephone to the Underworld. In greater detail, however, it describes Demeter's reactions to the loss of her child.

Unbeknown to Demeter, Persephone is abducted and ravished by her brother, Hades, King of the Underworld. That act is both planned and implemented under the aegis of Zeus, the girl's father. Although not with her when the kidnapping occurs, Demeter hears Persephone's cries. For nine days she tries unsuccessfully to identify the perpetrator. Receiving no help, Demeter meets Hekate. That goddess relates hearing the child's screams, but is unable to give Demeter the name of the abductor. Finally the distraught mother learns from Helios of the collusion between Zeus and Hades. Learning of the circumstances surrounding the abduction, Demeter, the "goddess of ripeness and giver of rich gifts,"[4] plunges further into grief. She leaves Olympus in the disguise of an elderly woman, and travels among mortals. While resting at the Well of the Virgin near the palace of King Keleos,

Demeter is approached by Keleos' four daughters. She mumbles her name to them, and explains that she was captured by pirates from whom she has escaped. She inquires about the possibility of a position within the palace doing housework and child care. The girls approach their mother, Lady Metaneira, and the goddess is given responsibility for raising Demophoön, the newly born son. Maintaining her disguise, Demeter rears the child lovingly. She feeds him ambrosia and at night exposes him to fire in order to burn off aspects of his mortality. By accident, Metaneira observes the old woman's behavior and, in terror, interferes.

Demeter feels rage toward the Queen and lays the child down. She admits having prepared Demophoön for immortality, but because of human ignorance, he and the other men of Eleusis would be forever at war and would come to know death. Showing herself to be a powerful goddess, Demeter orders the King to construct a temple in her honor wherein she continues to grieve and to cause famine throughout the land. Zeus and many other gods implore her to allow the earth to blossom again. In anger, she refuses all such exhortations, and demands to see her daughter.

At last, Zeus sends Hermes to the Underworld in order to reunite mother and daughter. That prospect thrills Persephone, and she leaves Hades' realm willingly. Prior to her departure, Hades feeds her three pomegranate seeds, ensuring her return for a third of each year. She remains with her mother the rest of the year.

What makes Demeter a mythic mentor?

Initiates at Stage II of the Re-Membering rite are vulnerable because parts of their well-honed identities must begin the dying process. They need to look to and to trust a mentor who identifies with and understands their circumstances. Of all the major goddesses, Demeter best meets that requirement. In fact, the word "vulnerable" has been ascribed to her as well as to Hera and Persephone. Jean Shinoda Bolen describes these three goddesses as ones whose identities and well-beings depend on having a significant relationship "... [they] were raped, abducted, dominated, or humiliated by male gods. Each suffered when an attachment was broken or dishonored. Each experienced powerlessness."[5]

When I read about Demeter's personality, I benefitted not only from her practical experience as a consummate caretaker, but also from her divine wisdom. Through her example, I was able to complete the tasks associated with this stage: to expose my dying parts and to grieve their passing.

Karl Kerenyi states that to know Demeter fully one needs "to be pursued, robbed, raped, fail to understand, rage and grieve, but then get everything back and be born again."[6] The way in which I chose to view Demeter's transformation was as that of maternal martyr to mature adult. As the most nurturing of all goddesses, Demeter was susceptible to victimization. At birth, she was swallowed by her father; she was raped by her brother/consort, and she was betrayed by her child's father.

As one of Demeter's followers in Stage II of the Re-Membering rite, you must excise the part of your intrapsychic self that I call "Helpless Victim." Like Demeter, infant girls in our society are swallowed up, betrayed, and raped by the lopsided mandates found in patriarchal constructs. In the simple act of growing up, many girls forfeit their feminine attributes and strengths. They become innocent victims of our society's exaltation of masculine values. To Demeter and to her Re-Membering contemporaries of the '90s, the cost of growing up amid patriarchal mandates is high. An environment that lionizes imbalanced perspectives and beliefs causes a young woman's sense of worth to diminish and her sense of victimization to escalate. Cultural dichotomies or polarities reinforce that tendency. They confuse relatedness with dependency, couple care to emotionality, and translate emotionality as irrationality or weakness.

In her hymn, Demeter exposes her role of potential victim. She assumes that persona in some of her initial reactions to Persephone's abduction. By pining, yearning, crying, raging, and falling into depression, Demeter expresses her feelings, but remains unsuccessful in capturing the attention of Zeus, the perpetrator. Not until she withdraws her feminine powers to create, those associated with her image as bountiful Earth Mother, does Demeter create movement toward the realization of her goal of reunification with her daughter. Demeter's internalized image as victim dies when she finds her real locus of control and decides to use it.

Through Demeter's example, I was able to unmask the "Helpless Victim" in myself. As I conversed with it, I discovered that this aspect of my personality consisted of many "martyred mes": the parentified golden child, the tragic young widow, the self-surrendering single mom, the betrayed businesswoman, the emotionally-battered lover, and finally, the culturally-fractured female. As each of those roles was dying, it described its origin and called me its "mother." Over several months, I listened respectfully to the voices of my various selves. At last I was able to assume full responsibility for creating and nurturing them. At that point, I had acquired sufficient strength and confidence to thank each aspect of my victimized self for guiding me inward. Then I was able to bless it, and let it go.

The second part of my theoretical identity that I exposed during Stage II was that of the "Perfect Mom." While several other goddesses within the pantheon bore children, Demeter is identified as being the consummate mother. It was her relationship with Persephone that most greatly influenced the goddess' sense of identity. As a mother, a single mom at that, Demeter executed her maternal responsibilities with love, openness, patience, and support. Demeter's roles as biological mother of Persephone, bountiful mother to mankind, and spiritual mother to her followers at Eleusis were top priorities in her life.

I am certain that following Persephone's abduction Demeter was tormented by feelings of self-blame, shame, and guilt. I am not surprised that she succumbed to depression. The daughter into whom her identity was intimately spun had been kidnapped under the aegis of the child's father. Suddenly, Demeter's nest was empty and so were her mind and heart. I can visualize the goddess beating her breast and lamenting, "If only I had been there … If only I hadn't been so trusting … If only I had been more vigilant!" Those feelings can easily become commiserating companions to any initiate walking her path as "Perfect Mom."

I had to come to grips with this compassionate culprit. She proved to be a tough negotiator, though, and threatened to delay my inner journey or cause it to be cancelled altogether. For years, I had naively accepted her persuasive propaganda. For example, I believed that a good mom did everything, an even better mom would never say "no," and the best mom of all sacrificed her own needs for those of her children, parents, spouse, boss—even of members of the in-house menagerie.

After I exposed my "Perfect Mom" and spoke with her, I realized how she had become the principal actress in my life's drama. Especially as a young widow, "Perfect Mom" felt compelled to overcompensate her abandoned daughter for having experienced one of life's cruelest cuts. The child who had shared my body and blood was, at four months, branded with a "G" for grief, "an invisible scar that every now and then burned."[7] Although the umbilicus was cut at birth, the cord that united us emotionally remained intact. Over the years, my façade of "Perfect Mom" had taken a high toll on my well-being. It had placed the relationship I had with my daughter in bondage and created a no-win situation for both of us. When I admitted that "Perfect Mom" was dying, I recall feeling sad and guilty. Along with her death rattle, I heard "Perfect Mom's" final admonishments: "How dare you! You are being selfish. You should be ashamed. You'll be sorry!" Over several long and labored months, I panted and pushed her out of the leading role she had assumed in my life. During that time, I was helped by visualizing the maternal cord that connected me to my ancient authentic self—my feminine soul.

The third Great Pretender within me that had to be exposed and sacrificed was my "Masterful Male." During my dialogue with him, I learned that I had chosen to follow his lead quite early in life. By striving hard to meet the demanding expectations of his tutelage, he expected that I distance myself from that which was the deep, feminine part of myself. In fact, I became convinced that some of those very qualities were impediments to my attaining happiness and success. "Masterful Male" taught me new language and behaviors that would help me "make it" in a man's world. That language included the words: feminine, success, sexuality, intimacy, maturity, adulthood, normal, power, relationship, and dependency. I found that his operational definitions of those terms were used in educational institutions, business organizations, family structures, and even churches. He showed me how to maneuver through those varied domains by overachieving, being perfect, and acquiring a sense of personal power through financial independence and psychological separation.

My encounter with him was the most difficult and conflicted. I detested him for raping my psyche and for betraying my trust. However, I feared letting him die because I had grown so dependent upon him. I relied on his eyes, ears, and brain to perceive my Superwoman's world. Also, I feared society's possible retributions were I to make "Masterful Male" a sacrificial offering in my mid-life ritual. He never fully accepted responsibility for the accusations I leveled against him. I guess he just could not understand. My final words to him were, "Thank you for preparing me to exist in a man's world, but to live there, I must acknowledge and celebrate the womanly part of myself."

Demeter, then, is an appropriate mentor for initiates in Stage II for these reasons: 1) she guides women in exposing the parts of themselves they must surrender; and 2) she teaches them how to grieve. Demeter is called the "Grieving Mother"[8] because, when she lost her maternal role, life itself lost its meaning. At that point, Demeter embodied grief, as must Re-Membering women who are at this stage of their midlife rite of passage.

Grief is a universal and natural response to loss. It can become more intense and prolonged when that loss represents something of great personal value: for example, a child or a part of oneself. As an experience, grief has many characteristics: it is painful, bound by cultural and religious beliefs, ageless, genderless, and multi-dimensional; that is, grief is felt by body, mind, heart, and soul.

While Demeter encourages an initiate to grieve, it is the individual woman who must give herself permission to feel and to act out her grief. In Stage II, participants can expect to experience a number of grief-related feelings and behaviors. Once they have accepted the reality of their wounds, their anger may move from mild resentment to full-fledged rage. Sorrow may run the course between disappointment and depression. Finally, participants may also confront the feelings of guilt and shame while in this stage of the Re-Membering rite. For example, they may be ashamed of how they are managing their grief, or plagued by thoughts of self-centeredness. Jacquelyn Small states "Selfishness is a stepping stone to Self-ness."[9] She goes on to reframe the concept of selfishness by suggesting that neither men nor women can give to someone else something they do not possess themselves; therefore, they must develop and share that which is true within themselves. As mythic mentor, Demeter epitomized her Self-ness as she grieved in ways that were neither muted nor muffled.

What are some of Demeter's qualities?

I have already touched upon some of Demeter's positive character traits, including her honesty, openness, and expressiveness. In addition to those, the goddess with the beautiful hair[10] exhibits within herself the gifts of nurturance, tenacity, and generosity.

The word "nurture" carries more than one connotation: to supply with nourishment; to educate, and to foster.[11] Examples of each definition become evident in Demeter's, or practically any mother's, personal mythology. Not only did she provide physical nourishment to Persephone, but Demeter also educated humankind in the art of nurturing themselves; that is, planting and harvesting grain. While she stayed in Keleus' house, Demeter also nourished his little son, Demophoön, as if he were her own. She even fed him ambrosia as a way to prepare his physical body for immortality. Finally, the goddess fed the souls of those who followed her spiritual teachings as conveyed in the Eleusian Mysteries.

Most women at midlife have acquired a post-graduate degree in nurturance. With little formal training, we feed, educate and cherish the bodies, minds, and spirits of those we have woven into our relational webs. Oftentimes, as Demeter's maternal alchemy works through us, we bring out that which is highest in others. Because of the painful tasks they must accomplish in Stage II, initiates need to learn a new pattern surrounding their gift of nurturance: they must extend it to themselves.

It was at this stage of the Re-Membering process that I looked to Demeter to teach me about nurturing myself. Her domain was that of the middle realm, the heart. It seemed to me as if my heart had always beat effortlessly while meeting the needs and desires of others. When focusing on self-care, though, my heart muscle almost atrophied and was in dire need of stretching.

As maternal archetype, Demeter's heart-centeredness spoke to me of the qualities of rhythm, love, and balance. I realized that in order to find my True Self, I had to make time in the daily flow of life for me. I had to observe the rhythms of life, both around and in me, in order to establish and maintain a routine that offered me visibility and validity. The external cycles seen in the change of seasons or in the movement of the moon and stars, as well as my own internal monthly cycle, helped me acquire a newfound sense of security. By systematically placing me within my day's rhythm, I established a time and place that belonged just to me.

Another lesson about nurturance that flowed naturally from Demeter's maternal heart concerned love. The initiate's capacity to enfold others in her blanket of maternal love is a powerfully creative force. Somehow, in Stage II, I had to learn to apply to myself the pure and selfless love that I felt instinctively toward my daughter. As I broke down and surrendered long-held and much-admired aspects of my identity, I discovered that those Great Pretenders had lessened my ability to experience the precious gift of self-love. In fact, they engendered self-rejection and even self-hate. Following their criteria of acceptability, my self-assessment always contained far more deficits than assets.

Finally, the goddess' heart-centered consciousness helped me become more balanced. As I exposed the fraudulent parts of my identity, then watched them die, I became painfully aware of several unhealthy imbalances in my life: work over play, other's needs over mine, past time over present, outer development instead of inner, and masculine values instead of feminine. My attempts at becoming better balanced proved to be creative stratagems that healed wounds from the past, eased pain in the present, and radiated hope into the future.

Yet another positive attribute ascribed to Demeter is that of persistence. She refused to relinquish her dream of reunification with Persephone, even when she was pulled into the underground of her own depression. Stage II may present particularly painful tasks to the initiates. At times, you may consider giving up your midlife journey. Your heartache may become too great, family dynamics may change too dramatically, or transition time may be just too long. Demeter encourages you "to hang in there."

In her mythology, Demeter exhibits a third quality that benefits Re-Membering women in the Dying Stage of their personal unfoldment. They need to experience the support of other women and share their innate wisdom and strengths. Resembling a very old woman, the disconsolate Demeter was resting on a road in Eleusis. She was near the Well of the Fair Dancers when the daughters of Keleus invited her into their home as nurse to their little brother. With a gracious heart, Demeter accepted the invitation. On an abstract level, the four daughters and Demeter found refreshment, shared it, and were replenished by it at the well of their feminine psyche.

In addition to several positive qualities, there are a few Demetrian traits that may impede a woman's progress through the Dying Stage of her midlife rite. Those include her tendency to nurture others and not herself, her fostered dependency on those parts of her identity that she must surrender, her lack of assertiveness on her own behalf, and her depression.

As I have already explained, a participant must learn and implement a different pattern concerning her strong instinct to nurture. Instead of finding another person or cause to embrace, the initiate has to feel entitled to her own nurturance. In the spirit of becoming self-responsible, she must learn to provide herself with "the goodies" she has lavished on others.

A Demetrian follower needs to be aware of just how dependent she has grown on the parts of her personality from which she must separate. The root system extending from those various public images may have grown thick and deep into her consciousness. As she tries to release them, she may be plagued by feelings of insecurity and incompetence. Questions such as "Who will I be?" and "What will I do?" may become roadblocks on her path of personal development.

Demeter never directly confronted Zeus about his role in their daughter's abduction. Feeling frustrated, resentful, angry, and powerless, she continued to search for Persephone. At length, Demeter became noncompliant; that is, she refused to do what was expected of her. Zeus had failed to take her seriously. As a last resort, she gained his attention by "going on strike." After exposing the Self-denying parts of yourselves, you must explore how those aspects of your sculpted identities either ignored or demeaned your real needs and desires.

Finally, in Stage II, as your own intrapsychic nests empty of images "mothered" over decades, you may fall into a depression. Like Demeter, you might become withdrawn and unresponsive, and your psychological and spiritual growth may seem to have stopped. As the initiate gives herself to grief, it is important that she accept responsibility for her wellness. Should you become overwhelmed by negative feelings, you need to seek support actively—perhaps through professional intervention.

Stage II Tasks and Strategies

There is one prominent goal that initiates strive to meet in Stage II: to surrender parts of their known identity for unknown ones. In order to do this, you have to master the tasks involved in consciously dying and grieving. At this stage of your Re-Membering rite, you may find it helpful to employ some or all of the strategies described below:

- ✧ Get to know yourself better. Become further acquainted with your internal root system and external anchors. Consider who and what is of value to you. Next, prioritize that list.
- ✧ Think about the various subpersonalities or roles that compose your public image. Give each one a name: for example, the mother, the critic, the advocate, the wife, the maid, the perfectionist. Decide whether each role reflects your theoretical self or your True Self. How can you capitalize on those that mirror authenticity? Which one(s) are Great Pretenders and need to die in order for you to find your True Self?
- ✧ Seek and use a network of professional and/or peer support. Name some people you already know who would be understanding and empathetic.

- Let go of those parts of your public image that must die. This may take a lot of time and hard work. It is important to express honestly the feelings you hold toward each one. Consider your level of personal dependency surrounding them. In a journal, dialogue with each one to discover how it originated and how you incorporated it into your life.
- Find out how you feel about mothering yourself. What kind of nurturing do you receive from others and yourself? How do you integrate your needs and desires into your daily or weekly rhythm?

  What balance exists in your life between mothering others and mothering yourself? What is your primary method of sabotaging self-care?
- Grieve the death of parts of your old self honestly. Schedule time to do your grief work. Give yourself permission to express all of your feelings, and be gentle with yourself.
- Make a commitment to yourself and perhaps to some other supportive person to continue your personal Re-Membering rite.
- Become accustomed to listening for your inner voice, then follow the advice that is given. This means that you must clear your inner communication waves of "outside static," then trust that such guidance will be forthcoming from deep within yourself.

Stage II's Major Obstacle

The midlife rite of Re-Membering is about reclaiming an authentic sense of Self. For women, that means reconnecting with the feminine part of our psyches from which we probably separated as we pursued contemporary symbols of success and happiness. Women in Stage II need to hold tight to their goal of discovering wholeness through becoming authentic. At this point, the theoretical image of myself that I had created and embraced over decades had to be purified. It is important to underscore the fact that my theoretical self was not bad, only that it was an illusion.

The primary impediment to progress at this stage of personal unfoldment is fear. For me, the act of purification generated a variety of fears: fear of the probable pain, fear of the unknown, fear of disapproval, fear of becoming nothing. To move through the Dying Stage, an initiate must make a conscious decision to expose those fraudulent parts of her persona, confront all of her associated fears, then sacrifice them. Jacquelyn Small says that "fear is an ego defense based on illusion."[12] An identity that is anchored to sand is just as illusive. My Great Pretenders distorted perceptions that I held not only of myself but also of other people and things in my life.

For the vulnerable "midlifer," letting go of the string that has attached her to an identity is scary. Fear is a natural response at this stage of the Re-Membering process. What is important is how she will best manage that fear. That choice and responsibility rest with her.

A Reflective Exercise

What the initiate is asked to do in this stage of her personal journey is monumental. Completing the tasks will take time so you must be patient with yourself. These exercises are designed to help you do your work. I suggest that you write your responses in a journal. Also, it may be beneficial to discuss some of them within the parameters of a supportive relationship.

a) Let strands of your memory follow your root system back into its origin in early or latent childhood. Ask yourself: What are my beliefs and values? Where are they rooted? What do I value in being female? To what people, concrete things, and abstract objects have I anchored my identity? Meditate upon those questions for as long as you need. Which anchor points reinforce your sense of True Self? Which ones reflect your manufactured or theoretical self?

b) Think about how (or if) you practice self-care and how you integrate balance into your daily or weekly routine. Make four columns on your journal page and label them: Body, Mind, Heart (feelings), Spirit. Under each heading, list ways in which you nurture yourself. Read over your self-care inventory. Is there an imbalance evident? Think about different strategies you employ to sabotage your own self-care. Journal about any feelings, thoughts, or insights you may have.

c) Close your eyes and become comfortable riding the waves of your own breathing. Just BE for awhile. Then ask yourself: Who am I? Focus on your perception of all the various roles you assume during the course of a day. Who are the different actors/actresses that regularly execute your life script? You may envision them realistically, as abstract symbols, or as words. When you feel ready, transfer your thoughts and images of your self-portrait into your journal. When you finish your drawing, study it and ask it to talk to you. Ask the different subpersonalities to name themselves. Which ones assume major roles in your life? Which are minor players? Which reflect your True Self? How did the others originate? Which ones must leave your psychic nest at this time in your personal development?

d) Ask yourself this question: What are my attitudes toward dying and grief? Write those two key words at the top of your journal page. Below each one, write words that simply pop into your head. Be spontaneous. Read over your responses and try to identify any themes that recur. Also, journal any feelings or thoughts that may have surfaced as you completed this exercise.

e) Reflect upon events in your life that have caused you to grieve. Visualize memories surrounding both the events and your reactions. Ask yourself: How does my body, mind, heart, and soul grieve such episodes? Answer that question by drawing a picture of your grieving self. Allow your perception of that part of yourself to come through in your sketch. When you have finished, study it. Let the picture describe itself to you. Journal about any feelings or thoughts that have surfaced as you completed this exercise. Also, think about answers to these questions: When you grieve, do you allow all feelings to surface, even anger and rage? What feelings do you experience? How do you act? Do you stay with your grief? How do you anesthetize your pain?

f) Close your eyes and ask yourself: What do I really fear at this time in my life? How is my fear expressed in everyday activities and relationships? Do my dreams provide insight into my fear? Meditate upon your most challenging fear, then transfer the image you hold of it onto your journal page. Title your drawing. Study it, then look beyond it to its "flip side," courage. What is one courageous step you can choose to take within the near future to minimize the impact of that fear on your life?

Ritual for Stage II: Exposing the Theoretical Self and Letting It Die

Having unmasked parts of your identity that have been blocking the energy flowing from your True Self, you are now ready to create a ritual that helps you let go of them and reinforces your authenticity. The major theme that underlies this ritual is purification, and it incorporates the acts of dying and grieving. Do not be overly eager to ritualize the closure of this stage. To do so prematurely might cause challenges for you later. Keep in mind that ghosts of your Great Pretenders will probably rise from the dead and tempt you to retreat into your former sense of self. They controlled much of your perception for a long time and may stalk you throughout the rest of your Re-Membering rite.

Prepare your body, mind, and heart for the ritual by taking several deep abdominal breaths. With each breath, imagine yourself exhaling the spirits of your Great Pretenders and inhaling air that will nurture and energize new life.

SEED THOUGHT:

To live authentically, I must move beyond well-established definitions of myself and follow the primal rhythms inherent in dying and grieving.

Know that your body, mind, and heart are eager to participate in this stage of your transformative journey. If you decide to follow any part of this suggested ritual, you will need to assemble some or all of the following materials: a candle, matches, a dish of salted water, some planting soil or local dirt, a smudge stick (sage), and some thread or string.

Having prepared your "sacred space," acknowledge the beginning of your ritual with a gesture, prayer, song, or reading of your choice.

As you light the candle, bring to mind the eternal light that indwells you. It is your source of true illumination. Affirm not only the purifying quality of fire but also its holy function of bringing light into darkness.

Bond yourself to the grounded nature of Demeter by either touching your forehead to the floor or by holding a handful of moist, living earth for a few minutes. As you seek your True Self, know that your roots draw nourishment from deep within your feminine nature.

Invoke the power and wisdom of Demeter. Allow your creative gift of imagination to breathe life into the goddess, then feel her presence. You may choose to use some of these invocations:

Invocations

Demeter, help me to separate from my old sense of self.

Demeter, encourage me to be true to my grief.

Demeter, give me the courage to continue my Re-Membering rite.

Demeter, teach me how to mother myself.

Demeter, honor me with your earth wisdom concerning balance, change, and rhythm.

Light your smudge stick and slowly trace a large circle around yourself and outline your entire figure with it. Bring to mind each part of your identity that must be sacrificed. For each one, say the following:

(Name of the subpersonality or role),
I bless you, but release you in the name of my True Self.

Turn counterclockwise in a full circle before you name the next subpersonality.

Pick up your dish of salted water and recognize it as being of the same composition as your tears. Sprinkle a few drops on your face and/or on other parts of your body. Do this three times.

Allow yourself the gift of silence for a few moments.

To remind yourself that parts of your familiar identity are dying, band yourself; that is, tie a piece of string or thread around one of your fingers. Know that you have chosen to die consciously, but that the act will require time, commitment, and grief.

Your band will help you be patient and honest with yourself.

Close your ritual in a way that feels comfortable to you.

You may want to journal your thoughts and feelings following this ritual. Also, it may be appropriate and necessary to conduct this ritual or variations of it several times in the future.

SUMMARY

STAGE II: THE WOUNDS

NATURE GUIDE
A banded tree

MYTHIC MENTOR
Demeter

MENTOR QUALITIES
Honest
Expressive
Nurturing
Maternal
Balanced
Persevering
Strong
Able to enlist support

PRIMARY TASK
To surrender the known identity for the unknown and to grieve the former.

PRIMARY STRATEGIES
Become self-observant
Identify sub-personalities
Network with peers
Become familiar with root system
Grieve honestly
Listen to inner voice
Nurture yourself

MAJOR OBSTACLE(S)
Fear

RITUAL FOCUS
Purification

WHOM MIGHT YOU ENCOUNTER?
Your Great Pretenders

I don't know what to look for inside of me. I don't know how to identify that I'm feeling something, let alone give a name to it. I think I've been anesthetized, deadened.

Alice Koller
A Woman Unknown

STAGE THREE: THE DEATH

NATURE GUIDE: A DEAD FISH

Here is a guide I tried to ignore. In fact, I walked twice around Lake Como one day in August in search of an appropriate alternative. For a long time, parts of me were resistant to acknowledging and honoring the wisdom to be found within the decomposing body of a fish that lay in shallow water just in front of my sacred spot. Finally, I listened to my intuition and whispered, "Teacher, I feel uncomfortable, but I will try to be receptive." After that, thoughts came in rushes.

"Don't be afraid to look into Death's face. Come closer. Smile at what you behold, for in Death's watery mirror is your own reflection.

"Death is no more than the interlude between each in-breath and out-breath. Think of it as being a totally safe process not unlike disrobing, dissolving, or melting away. Death would like her dance partners to be both alert and trusting. Alice was fully conscious as she plummeted down her tunnel to Wonderland. So too, you must consciously melt into the ambiguous cloud that will envelop you for some time to come. Trust that your life will become 'curiouser and curiouser.' Be open to the teachings of each moment because they are magic. During this time of timelessness, just BE!

"As the flesh becomes unglued from my bones, I am liquifying back into my birth cradle. You must do the same. As you navigate through this death-like stage, try to be both the observer and the observed self. Already you have peeled away parts of your externally-defined identity and have felt the pain caused by separation from your feminine nature. Allow the grace of self-forgiveness to illuminate your darkness and eliminate death's chill."

After my thoughts stopped, I felt an invisible bubble surround me. For a long time, I sat enclosed within a fourth dimension where time ticked by unnoticed.

The first idea to penetrate my bubble was that of a dream I had been having over the past several months. I would be standing at my kitchen window looking out onto the backyard. There, I would catch sight of a small, fenced-in area in which I kept my pet, a large, brown, lop-eared rabbit. One segment of the fence would always be knocked to the ground. The intruder, a red fox, would stare defiantly at me from within the enclosure. At its feet lay my dead bunny.

After the first time I had that dream, I sensed that my pet was feminine in gender and the fox was masculine. Also, I knew that both were aspects of myself. The masculine part, however, had overtaken the feminine. It always felt to me as if the fox were daring me to approach and overtake him. I would awaken to a variety of feelings: sadness, anger, and fear.

In that dream scene, I saw part of myself as the helpless victim, murdered by a stronger, more cunning predator. Now my imagination created a similar picture; one in which my physical body, dressed for success and power, was lying in state. For a moment I assumed the posture of both observer and observed. At that point, I understood fully what my guide had said to me. I paid homage to the deceased for the person she strove to be, as well as for what she had accomplished. I felt confused, however. Somehow, I was detached from that body, yet connected eternally to it at the heart. I wanted to sing about her fine qualities, celebrate her successes, and dance to the intricate rhythms she had executed during her just-lived life.

The tunnel through which I had begun to fall was dark and long. It turns out to have been the darkest and longest passageway I have experienced thus far in my life. It took me on a mind-bending journey out of my head down into the deepest recesses of my heart. There, at the center, I rediscovered my birthing bed.

The Goddess Guide: Hestia

What is Hestia's genealogy?

Hestia was the first daughter born to Rhea and Kronos. Kerenyi points out that as such "... she became both the youngest and the oldest since she was the first to be devoured by her father and the last to be yielded up again."[1] This means that Hestia not only spent the longest period of time in the darkness of her father's bowels, but also that she was the only one of his offspring to spend any time there in solitude. She was eldest sister to Demeter, Hera, Hades, Poseidon, and Zeus, and the maiden aunt to members of the second generation of Olympians. In time, Hestia's position within the canon of twelve was assumed by Dionysus.

What is Hestia's mythology?

In Greece, Hestia was worshiped as the goddess of the hearth and sacred tire. In fact, her name is derived from the Greek word meaning "hearth" or more specifically "of the fire burning on the round hearth."[2] Mythology surrounding this powerful goddess is meager, but her divine presence throughout Hellenic (and Roman) history becomes apparent through the role of the hearth and the sacred fire. Morford and Lenardon describe Hestia's relationship to those elements: "Among primitive men, fire was obtained with difficulty, kept alive, and revered for its basic importance in daily needs and religious ceremony. The hearth too was the center of the family and then of the larger political units, the tribe, the city, and the state. Transmission of the sacred fire from one settlement to another represented a continuing bond of sentiment and heredity. Thus the domestic and communal hearth were designated as holy, and the goddess herself presided over them."[3] Jean Shinoda Bolen states that a Hestian presence via hearth and fire symbolized "continuity and relatedness, shared consciousness and common identity."[4]

According to scholars, Hestia was one of three goddesses who was never swayed by Aphrodite's power. In fact, in some tales, the "alchemical goddess"[5] arranged for Hestia to be wooed by both Poseidon and the younger god, Apollo. After siding with her brother Zeus against their father and the Titans, however, Hestia made two requests of her brother: She should be allowed to remain virginal, and she should "receive not only the first but the last sacritice at every ceremonial assembly of mortals."[6] Those wishes were granted and her brother's response appears in this brief segment of "the Hymn to Aphrodite":

> *Zeus gave Hestia a beautiful privilege instead of a wedding gift; he had her sit in the center of the house or temple to receive the best offering's.*[7]

Mythologically, Hestia appears to have remained detached from divine and earthly intrigues and excesses. Instead of socializing, she chooses to remain close to her homely circle, the hearth. Hestia becomes "mystically mated," however to Hermes. Bolen suggests that these two deities represent the female and male principles and that, for a time, a "complementary duality"[8] existed between the August goddess and the clever god. While Hestian fires warmed Greek homes and created a sense of community, herms, phallic-shaped pillars with Hermes' head sculpted at the top, designated property, prosperity, and protection.

Finally, the mythology of Hestia would be incomplete were no mention made of the pagan Roman cult devoted to her. Vesta was worshiped in a circular temple built to honor the goddess of the hearth and goddess of chastity. Within that temple, the sacred fire was tended constantly by six Vestal Virgins. These women entered into the goddess' service sometime before their tenth year, and they were trained in the sacred teachings and rites. As part of the initiation into this esteemed station, each virgin took the vow of chastity, realizing that if it were ever broken, she would be buried alive.

What makes Hestia a mythic mentor?

William Bridges refers to the mid-point of his transitional model as "the time between the old life and the new," and he labels it, "The Neutral Zone."[9] I call this pivotal stage of the Re-Membering rite "The Death" because it represents a state wherein the initiate's once-vital sense of identity ceases to function. It was at this critical juncture that I was unaware of what was either alive or dead in me. I sensed Azriel's dark angelic presence and chose to accept Hestia's tutelage. For me, the Goddess of the Hearth and Temple best met the job description of mythic mentor at Stage III. She embodied wholeness, embraced solitude, linked past to the present, epitomized womanly wisdom, and represented a spiritual presence.

As I reread entries in my Re-Membering journals, I discovered that vocabulary often indicated my position in the transition process. Descriptors such as dissected, shredded, frozen, invisible, and dead appearing more frequently substantiated my hunch that I was immersed in the act of dying unto my former self. At that time, I empathized fully with the catastrophic circumstances that befell poor old Humpty Dumpty. Like him, I had taken a great fall. My fragile shell had been shattered and I felt that my insides had seeped out. I looked to Hestia for help in putting myself back together again. Luckily for me, she was more successful than all the king's horses or men had been with Humpty.

When I first read about Hestia, this thought kept popping into my head: "she really has her act together." Her symbol, the circle, illustrated what I perceived as a demeanor of intactness. In spite of participating in a patriarchal system, she was committed to being true to herself. I found that I envied her that stance and longed to feel a similar sense of wholeness. As a mentor, Hestia taught me about "psychological virginity" and its role in my Re-Membering rite of passage.

Because she had never engaged in sexual intercourse with either god or mortal, Hestia was virginal in the literal sense. Following her example, Hestia's followers are challenged to return to a virginal state of consciousness with respect to how they define themselves; that is, they need to contact the part of themselves that remains forever unsullied, chaste, and fresh. That discovery is part of the transformational adventure that unfolds in Stage III. One Hestian tool that unearths such treasures buried deep within a woman's feminine psyche is solitude.

The word, solitude, means "the quality or state of being alone or remote from society."[10] Contemporary semantics ascribes rather negative connotations to that word, suggesting the lifestyle of a recluse, hermit, or extreme introvert. I had always associated the image of a monastic contemplative with the concept of solitude. Hestia broadened my understanding of the word and showed me how to integrate it into the "busy-ness" of my daily routine. In spite of being spiritually present in all homes and temples, she knew how to be alone. According to Morford and Lenardon, "... when other gods went to a feast, Hestia alone stayed home."[11] Paradoxically, she related to the outside world by being focused inward and honoring her need for solitude.

Jean Shinoda Bolen points out: "Almost everyone experiences periods of unchosen solitude during their lives. Such periods usually begin with loss, grief, loneliness, and longing to be with others."[12] The Re-Membering initiate, having just experienced the death of her theoretical self, needs to make a conscious decision to practice the art of solitude. Within that silent sacred space she reflects upon herself, and this facilitates self-renewal. Because of the intense pain and fear that I felt after sacrificing my Great Pretenders, I was the last person in whose company I wanted to be. In solitude, a silent call of reveille awakened all my bogey men. As a result, I fell easy prey to several of society's quick-fix injunctions: "Just keep yourself busy"; "It's best not to be alone at this time"; and, "You need to get back in the saddle." Hestia encouraged me to remain at my station, the hearth of my heart, and tend its eternal flame.

The third reason I have selected Hestia as the most appropriate mythic mentor for Stage III is that she represents a link between the past and the present. It was the ritualistic transmission of Hestia's fire from one home or community to a new one that provided residents with a sense of history and relationship. In this stage of transition, Hestia supports the initiate as she detaches from secure feelings, categories, and definitions she once held. The goddess then encourages her disciple to move into and become receptive to a new matrix of unknowingness. I recall asking myself, while in this stage of the Re-Membering process, life's bottom-line questions: Who am I? What am I doing here? Where am I going? In the darkness of that grave-like space, Hestia's flame allowed me to shadow-box with possible answers. It illumined the thread of authenticity that connected me temporally to whom I had been in the past, appeared to be in the present, and would become in the future.

As the eldest offspring born to Rhea and Kronos, Hestia assumed the role of mature and august sibling. As mentor, she is comfortable with her maturity and, as a result, trusts her feminine wisdom. According to Maureen Murdoch: "Very often during this period (mid-life) ... women identify with Hestia and find the Wise Woman Within."[13] For too long, I had ignored, muffled, or doubted my Wise Woman's voice. With gentle coaxing, Hestia encouraged me to set that voice free. Learning to hear and trust it, however, proved to be painful and difficult work. It made me feel awkward and vulnerable. Initially, memories of messages voiced by my Great Pretenders drowned out her tentative beckonings. With time and trust, my Wise Woman's voice grew both in confidence and in volume, especially in my dreams.

Frequently, during this stage of my Re-Membering, strong feminine symbols were woven into the fabric of my dreams. One of those was the spider. In one particular dream, I was standing alone in a large empty room. The ceiling and walls were covered with spider webs so thick that they resembled Spanish moss. Intuition told me that my task was to clear away all of the webs. I approached a corner of the ceiling and pulled down an armful of webbing. A beautiful shade of sky blue popped through the opening. On the second swipe, I found myself looking directly at a gigantic white furry spider. She mesmerized me, but I felt no fear. All I did was listen as she repeated, "I am your friend." I know that this amicable arachnoid symbolized my Wise Woman. Also, I interpret the large empty room as being the center or womb of my unconsciousness wherein dwells my True Self. Finally, the webs represented illusions created by my theoretical self that obstructed my vision of authenticity.

As I became more comfortable with Hestia's spider-like presence and more deeply entrenched in Stage III, I discovered that the goddess' sacred flame illumined my spiral journey inward and steadied my groping footsteps. As the line between mentor and mystic became evanescent, my Hestian sojourns into solitude took on a mystical aura. During such times, I retooled my spiritual heritage and reframed my understanding of love.

Hestia lived a mystical way of life; that is, one based upon intuition or spiritual insight. Her ultimate reality was connected neither to her physical senses nor to her intellect, but rather to an indestructible communion with her True Self. As I followed Hestia's sacred flame, I realized that a spiritual gnosis was driving me: an inner knowledge of my eternal and intimate relationship with God, who indwelled me and whom I was to love, honor, and obey. During daily meditations, I grew in the ability to overlook my peripheral vision. At last I was able to focus upon that paradoxical "still point" that detached me from everything outside of myself while connecting me inextricably to it. An important transformative tool for me was "to practice the presence"[14] of that part of myself which related directly to God. As Hestia was divinely "rooted" to the True Self located within her sacred hearth and fire, I discovered the roots of my authenticity buried under debris left from my theoretical self. Like the mythical Phoenix, the presence of God's female nature within me arose triumphant out of those ashes.

In Stage III, I began to reconstruct my identity using parameters of the spirit rather than those of the ego or personality. It was at that point that I began to reassess the scriptural mandate, "Love your neighbor as yourself." How could I love myself or anyone else when I failed to recognize, claim, and honor my True Self? As role model, Hestia urged me to tend the sacred flame within my body temple. Following her example forced me to strip myself of egotistic pretenses and defenses, feel compassion for my human frailties, and love myself unconditionally as God loves me. Prior to this stage of the Re-Membering rite, I considered myself to be a child of God. Following my metaphorical death, I knew that I was a participant in the organic process of becoming a mature adult in God's service.

What are some of Hestia's qualities?

In addition to those qualities that make her a most benefic mentor, Hestia exhibits other traits that facilitate an initiate's progress through this transformative phase of the Re-Membering rite. Some of those are a) her willingness to listen; b) her commitment to service; c) her ability to say "no"; d) her unhurried attitude toward time; e) her even-tempered nature; and f) her spirit of humility.

In Stage III, initiates need to heed the advice proffered by their indwelling Wise Woman. Before accomplishing that task, however, they must be able to hear her whispered wisdoms. Sitting in silence with their mentor will help participants fine-tune their sixth sense of auditory intuition. When practicing their listening skills, Hestia urges her followers to be patient after becoming centered within themselves. She urges them to be open and to become receptive channels of wisdom.

Along with her ability to listen, another Hestian quality to be cultivated by her followers is the goddess' service orientation. Her sacred flame burned in service to members of individual households, as well as to members of entire ancient communities. It was her fire that allowed Greek citizens to prepare their food, warm and illumine their homes, worship in their temples, and realize a sense of common heritage. The goddess served those who worshipped her through the sanctity of rituals. Sometime during Stage III, Re-Membering women may wish to emulate their mentor's pledge to service.

Evidently, Hestia felt comfortable in asserting herself by saying "no" when she deemed it necessary. In spite of being wooed by two powerful gods, the goddess maintained her deep-seated desire to remain single and virginal. She pleaded that case persuasively to Zeus and was successful. Women who have descended into the depths of Stage III need to hear themselves saying "no" to myriad demands and expectations placed upon them, not only by little and big people caught in their relational web, but also by outmoded tapes recorded by voices of their former selves.

Along with becoming more assertive in remaining true to themselves, Stage III women facilitate their own progress by modeling their mentor's psychologically serene attitude toward time. Jean Shinoda Bolen states: "When Hestia is present, a woman ... is neither on a schedule or 'putting in time.' Consequently, she is in what the Greeks called *kairos* time—she is participating in time."[15] Although Hestia's flame was reflexive—it illumined both the past and the future—it burned brightest in the present. The lesson here is for the initiate to focus on the now and claim many moments each day as her own. Those behaviors will serve to replenish her sense of centeredness and inner peace.

One of the most obvious Hestian qualities to emulate is the goddess' even-tempered nature. Through detachment, Hestia transcended the extremes and excesses prevalent in life outside her sacred sanctuary. Hestian equanimity is one trait to be cultivated in solitude.

Yet another quality demonstrated by Hestia is a natural by-product of Stage III activity. Her diminished sense of ego is a distinguishing feature of the goddess. That trait is not to be interpreted as a lack of self-esteem. To the contrary, Hestia's venerable status continued to increase, even after she surrendered her highly-visible position among the original members of the Olympiad and assumed a posture of near-anonymity. Stage III extends to initiates the opportunity to develop the Hestian trait of humility. The more a participant detaches from the theoretical self, the more diminished her ego becomes. Activities in this stage facilitate this outcome: focusing inward, cultivating solitude, as well as listening to and trusting the intuitive feminine voice.

Stage III Tasks and Strategies

The ultimate goal an initiate must reach in Stage III is to detach from her former identity and reunite with her True Self. In Stage II, you identified and sacrificed parts of the theoretical self that you created and nurtured over time. This phase of the transitional rite of passage demands that you reflect upon and pay proper respect to your former sense of self. Having attended a memorial service of sorts in honor of your former self, you will embark on an excruciatingly adventurous descent inward that will take you deep into the grave-like darkness of your own heart. Below are some specific things that you can do to help yourself:

- Create both a space and an atmosphere that is conducive to solitude and spend time there on a regular basis. At first you may feel cramped and uncomfortable in your self-reflective cocoon, but persevere.
- Take full responsibility for having manufactured your Great Pretenders, then forgive yourself for making them such prominent actors in your life script.
- Be flexible and patient about the amount of time you spend in Stage III. The darkness may become too prolonged and the feelings too intense, but DO NOT ABORT the time you spend in this stage. Tend your own sacred hearth and fire at an unhurried pace.
- Assume a perspective of reflexivity; that is, be willing to look back honestly at the person you were and the one you are at this point in your transformation.
- See yourself as a receptive channel for your Wise Woman and anticipate hearing her voice, especially during times of meditation or prayer.
- Expect a dramatic change in your sense of identity. Actually, you most likely employed this strategy in Stage II; however,

it is essential to be aware of it in Stage III. The catalyst for the significant shift is your detachment from the familiar definition you held of yourself.

- Seek out and join a women's support group. Because we are used to being rooted in relational webs, women facilitate their own development and healing by being in the presence of peers. We need each other as "empathic resonators."[16]

- Broaden your understanding of feminine spirituality by attending classes or reading books on the topic. Among the latter are *Life's Companion,*[17] *Diving Deep and Surfacing: Women Writers on a Spiritual Quest,*[18] *The Mother's Songs: Images of God the Mother,*[19] *The Feminine Mystic and Other Essays on Women and Spirituality,*[20] *Ordinary People as Monks and Mystics,*[21] and *Journal of a Solitude.*[22] You might also consider talking with a spiritual director.

- Expect to feel devoured by rage. Wrathful feelings may erupt so volcanically that they engender fear and surprise in you. It is essential, however, that you express your rage fully and freely. To do that, you may wish to seek the professional support of a trained counselor.

- Assess your listening and assertiveness skills. Observe your own attitudes and behaviors concering these two areas. Are you able to listen to others? Can you hear your inner voice? How do you sabotage listening to yourself/others? Are you able to say "no" without feeling guilty? In what circumstances are you assertive/unassertive?

Stage III's Major Obstacles

There were two primary reasons why I became stuck in Stage III: l) I failed to give myself adequate time to master the associated task; and, 2) I denied both the existence and the expression of my rage.

Long before I began my Re-Membering rite, the word "time" appeared on my ever-growing list of dirty four-letter words. Feeling hurried, harried, and hassled by it, I started to envision time as a malevolent abuser in my life. For several months, I held on tight to that image and dealt with time in ways that were quite un-Hestian. Mostly, I tried to control it—slowing it down with sleep and speeding it up with "have-tos."

After the death of my old way of being, I experienced gut-wrenching pain. Following that, the descent into my inner world filled me with feelings of disorientation, disillusionment, and depression. I longed to place short-term limits around the amount of time I would spend voluntarily in the dark and isolated crypt of my mind.

Always, at some level, I knew that my descent represented a sacred journey. Because of that knowledge, I rejected society's prescription to shorten the length of time I stayed there and to medicate the pain I experienced in that lonely place. Gradually, time was transformed into a teacher that befriended and advised me. In whispered repetitions I heard it say, "Take back the dark with your inner light!" At that point, I acquiesced to time's unhurried unravelling and allowed it to hyphenate my identity. Only when time stood still, letting me dangle between who I had been and who I was to become, did the roots and seed pods of my former self shrivel up and blow away. Thus released, I groped in the darkness for several months until, at last, I looked upon the feminine face of my True Self.

The second obstacle to my movement through Stage III was my reluctance, or perhaps my inability, to deal with repressed anger or rage. Profiling your typical "nice lady," I had been reared to sidestep anger and suppress rage. As a child, I began to equate anger with evil. Striving to maintain a "nice" atmosphere within the family system, I adopted the old adage, "See no evil, hear no evil, speak no evil," as my *modus operandi*. In her book, *The Dance of Anger*, Harriet Lerner says: "the more we are 'nice,' the more we accumulate a storehouse of unconscious anger and rage."[23] Ironically, it was not until I was surrounded by darkness that I began to see the light concerning my anger. From out of the blackest recesses of my psychological pit, a rageful ogress emerged. After demanding permission to be heard, my Suppressed Shrew began to vent her feelings of betrayal, fear, shame, and self-loathing.

Lerner goes on to explain that "Anger is inevitable … when we behave as if having a relationship is more important than having a self."[24] Growing up within a male-dominated society, most females follow the unspoken rule that Lerner labels "de-selfing"; that is, "negotiating too much of one's self (thoughts, wants, beliefs, ambitions) under pressures from relationships."[25]

My Suppressed Shrew raged at length about how, as a card-carrying member of the '80s superwoman cult, I had sacrificed too much of my feminine soul in the name and for the glory of the "ubiquitous other." The destructive force of her volcanic eruptions frightened me. I decided to seek professional intervention to help me understand, validate, and express my rage in healthy ways. Beginning with a six-day intensive workshop on anger, the Shrew spewed forth her molten madness. Through their expert guidance, the two facilitators helped me master new tools to unlearn old repressive habits and redirect "anger energy"[26] into Re-Membering myself.

Upon first encounter, I wanted to slay my rageful ogress because I saw her as wretched, repulsive, and evil. Little did I know that she was my personalized Vestal Virgin "in drag." It was her esteemed task to guard the door of my inner temple and to mind the flame of my sacred True Self. With patience, forgiveness, respect, and laughter, my relationship with her continues to change over time. Now, when she makes herself evident, I understand the dance we must do together, then defer the lead to my Adultwoman.

A Reflective Exercise

Before you begin these exercises, remind yourself of the enormous task that you have been dealing with in this stage of the Re-Membering rite: to detach from your theoretical self and to reunite with your True Self. Be certain to give yourself sufficient time to think about the exercises. Allow time to become your own advocate for authenticity. As before, you may choose to journal your responses and, at the appropriate time, discuss them with a supportive friend or counselor.

a) Close your eyes and see yourself attending your own memorial or funeral service. Though this exercise may feel uncomfortable, it is most appropriate for you to experience it at this time. After all, parts of your theoretical self have died and it is only right that you pay your respects. From the vantage point of a corner near the ceiling, activate all of your senses: smell the flowers, see your body, hear the music, prayers, and good-byes. How is your former self eulogized? What of its life is remembered? What is its legacy? What kinds of music or readings are included? What feelings do you experience as an invisible observer?

b) Write down the word "solitude." As freely as possible, allow words that you associate with solitude to flow through your mind and onto the paper. When you have finished, ask the words to speak to you. What do they tell you about attitudes you hold toward being alone?

c) Practice being both the observer and the observed. During a specific period of time that feels comfortable to you (one hour, day, week), document the amount of time you spend in solitude. After each episode, journal your feelings as well as thoughts and behaviors that either enhanced or obstructed your journey inward.

d) In your mind, image your Wise Woman. How does she look? What qualities does she possess? When do you hear her voice most clearly? What creates "static" in your communication with her? In writing, dialogue with her by considering these questions:

   How can you help me?

   How did you acquire your wisdom?

   How can I contact you?

   How can I learn to trust you?

   Why is it hard for me to hear you?

   How do you see me?

   What should I do about ______________________?

e) Hestia serves her followers as a role model for "being" instead of "doing." How do you relate to those two different ways of experiencing life? Are you able to BE yourself and be with yourself? When doing for yourself or others, are there strings of invisible expectations attached? How do these concepts relate to the formation, maintenance, and transformation of your identity?

f) Close your eyes and turn yourself inward. Think about how your Suppressed Shrew might look. What traits do you fear, dislike, or criticize in her? Does she ever have free reign over your feelings and behaviors? Under what circumstances does she express herself? You may want to sketch her portrait. Study her picture and acknowledge the part she plays in your self-acceptance and wholeness.

g) Mandala is an ancient Sanskrit word that means "to have possession of one's essence."[27] Frequently, a mandala is designed in the form of a circle. Hestia's symbol is the circle. As her follower, you may choose to create your own sacred circle.

   You will need a sheet of paper or a journal page, a pencil, a compass, crayons, colored pencils, or paints. Be certain to approach this exercise with a receptive and reverent attitude.

   Before you begin to draw, close your eyes and picture yourself in the center of the paper. Think about an image that represents your inner core or True Self. Next, bring to mind other qualities that emanate from your True Self.

   Slowly open your eyes. Using the compass, draw a circle to frame your mandala. Next, place a dot in the center of the page. Around that centerpoint, draw the image that symbolizes your unique True Self. Around that central image, draw the symbols of other qualities you envisioned.

   Finally, color your design. Allow the colors to choose themselves. When finished, study your mandala and journal your feelings and thoughts about it.

Ritual for Stage III: Eulogizing the Theoretical Self and Reclaiming the True Self

As I created and conducted rituals at different points throughout my Re-Membering rite of passage, I discovered that they announced, validated, and celebrated this fact: change was an eternal element in my life. Following each ritual, my perception of I AM, I CAN, and I WILL became clearer and more credible. In spite of feeling as if I had died, I was forced to acknowledge the eternal life-force within me that cried out to be acknowledged.

This stage of the Re-Membering process is about surrender and transcendence. Jacqueline Small states: "Surrendering has nothing to do with giving one's power over to an 'old man in the sky' out there somewhere ... Surrendering is not a negative statement about the Self, but a positive one: I am turning my life over to the Real Self that I've always been."[28]

As an impersonal observer, you will come to understand the need to surrender your theoretical self to Azriel, the angel of death. Then, as a spiritual seeker, you must accept and honor the authenticity of your True Self which aligns you with the feminine qualities of God, compels you toward wholeness, and transforms you into a valuable servant of humanity.

The purpose of this ritual is to help you comprehend the death of your ego-dominated view of self, commit it to an intrapsychic tomb, and reunite with your True Self. As I have stressed before, it is important for you to participate in a closing ritual that is personally meaningful to you. Read over this ritual and feel free to edit or enhance it in ways that your inner voice directs.

When you feel ready to begin, prepare the physical space in which you will conduct your ritual. Trace Hestia's symbol, the circle, around your "altar" and assemble all of the objects that will give meaning to what you are about to do. Should you decide to follow this ritual step-by-step, you will need these items: your mandala, a candle, matches, a song, poem, or reading that you enjoy, a listing of gifts, talents, and accomplishments attained by your theoretical self, a written obituary of that self, a dish of potting soil or dirt, and a small bowl of water.

First, cleanse your sacred space by sprinkling drops of water on the altar and in the four directions within your "Hestian hearth."

Next, enter into communion with your body, mind, and spirit by noticing the steady rhythm of your breath. At first, just be aware of it, then encourage it to become fuller and deeper. With each inhalation, breathe in that which affirms the True Self and breathe out all thoughts, values, and beliefs that have obstructed it in the past.

Light your ritual candle. Let its flame symbolize an inner "grow light" that nourishes your True Self and causes it to expand into consciousness. Read over this seed thought, then take it with you into several moments of silence:

SEED THOUGHT:

"i" have died and been buried. In time,
this sacred darkness will surrender to
the emergence of my Re-membered "I".

Pay homage to the whole of your theoretical self by playing a piece of music "she" especially liked or reading a favorite selection. With a sense of gratitude, read aloud the positive legacy left by your Synthetic Superwoman image: her gifts, strengths, skills, and accomplishments.

Now, acknowledge those aspects of your theoretical "i" that served the ego but obstructed your True "I." Help yourself detach from those parts by repeating this mantra:

Parts of me are dead.
I created, respected, and loved them.
Parts of me are dead.
I forgive, bless, and surrender them.

Finally, read aloud the obituary you wrote describing your Superwoman identity. Put a match to it and allow it to burn in the dish filled with dirt. After it has been consumed by fire, mix the ashes into the dirt. Affirm to yourself that she will rest in peace and that your Authentic Adultwoman will rise out of those ashes.

Visualize yourself seated at Hestia's hearth, tending her sacred flame. Know that, like your mentor, you have the ability to remain centered and thus, "taste and see the goodness of God" (Psalm 33). Invoke Hestia's presence with these thoughts:

Invocations

Hestia, help me seek my true nature.

Hestia, teach me detachment.

Hestia, encourage me to observe myself.

Hestia, keep me centered.

Hestia, comfort me in my solitude.

Hestia, guide me inward.

Hestia, direct me with your wisdom.

Pick up your mandala and focus your entire attention on it. Consider it to be the window to your feminine soul. Your Wise Woman has drawn forth the ancient symbols from deep within your unconscious mind. She has whispered their meaning to you as the lyrics of a heartsong. Play a favorite piece of joy-filled music. Meditate upon the seed of your Adultwoman that lies deep within, then give yourself over to a mental or physical dance of rediscovery. Celebrate!

Close your ritual with a gesture, prayer, or music.

SUMMARY

STAGE III: THE DEATH

NATURE GUIDE
A dead fish

MYTHIC MENTOR
Hestia

MENTOR QUALITIES
Virginal
Good listener
Comfortable with solitude
Centered
Able to say "No"
Humble
Even-tempered
Service oriented
Links past to future

PRIMARY TASK
To detach from former identity, honor it, and reunite with True Self

PRIMARY STRATEGIES
Become self-observant
Spend time in solitude
Network with peers
Listen to inner voice
Express feelings
Say "no"
Assess assertiveness skills

MAJOR OBSTACLE(S)
Time
Rage

RITUAL FOCUS
Surrender and Comprehension

WHOM MIGHT YOU ENCOUNTER?
Your Wise Woman
Your Suppressed Shrew

Everything is gestation and then bringing forth. To let each impression and each germ of a feeling come to completion wholly in itself, in the dark ... and await with deep humility and patience the birth-hour of a new clarity.

Rainer Maria Rilke
Letters to a Young Poet

STAGE FOUR: THE GESTATION

NATURE GUIDE: AN ACORN

This guide came to me as an unexpected gift. While vaulting from one arboreal tightrope to another, a bushy-tailed aerialist dropped an acorn into my sacred space. I picked it up and stared at it in the palm of my hand. The smooth brown face of a turbanned guru stared back, then said:

"You cradle me tenderly as if I were a fragile fleeting seed. Because of my size and humble appearance, you seem oblivious to the gifts of longevity, power, and strength that indwell me. This hard fibrous exterior is only a temporary receptacle that holds the genetic blueprint of my full potential.

"To realize the possibility of my True Self, I must endure a period of gestation within Mother Nature's dark fertile womb.

"During that time, she bonds with each seed-child. Maternal love forms a protective shield around us and encourages us to become all we might be. Gestation offers Mother Nature an unparalleled opportunity to shape the life-course of her progeny; that is, to bless us with the legacies of authenticity, autonomy, and acceptance.

"In a real sense, my friend, you are in a gestational state. Mentally, you are pregnant with the embryonic identity of your Adultwoman. Like mine, your external form is but a physical vessel that holds the wisdom, power, and glory that is truly you. Granted, your seed of True Self has accompanied you since the blink of your biological conception. It failed to thrive, however, because you detached yourself from it. Your attitude toward this pregnancy matters greatly, as it will influence your sense of happiness, well-being, and wholeness throughout the second half of your life.

"During this gestation, you must learn to function both as mother and midwife. As the former, you need to be aware of the special learning that takes place in the classroom of your intrapsychic womb. The developing seed of your Re-Membered identity is aware of and absorbs the curriculum that you design through your thoughts, feelings, and actions. I challenge you maternally in two ways: 1) to create a warm and emotionally enriching seedbed in which the identity of your Adultwoman will develop; and 2) to bond with it, using the maternal tools of affirming thoughts, honest feelings, unlimited patience, and unconditional love.

"As midwife, you must promote and defend these facts: 1) to be pregnant with the seed of one's authentic identity is a normal part of maturation at midlife; 2) to practice prenatal care is of prime importance; and 3) to hasten your due date is impossible.

"Now is your season of ripening. Take the yoke of responsibility upon yourself. Let the light of self-knowledge guide your growth with clarity, confidence, but most of all love."

I felt humbled by the wondrously simple wisdom my Guide had just shared. The idea of being pregnant with the seed of my Re-

Membered self was intriguing yet intimidating. Questions darted arrow-like across my mind:

> How did I really feel about this pregnancy?
>
> Will it change how I look, feel, and act?
>
> What will my Authentic Adultwoman be like?
>
> When will she be "born"?
>
> Will her birth be painful?
>
> How might I enhance or impede her development?
>
> Will other people in my life like her?

When I returned home, I studied myself in the mirror. The expression on my face confirmed the fact that bringing my True Self to term at midlife would be a joy-filled event. For several weeks, I chose to keep my "condition" to myself. Following a pattern of communication that I had established when pregnant with my daughter, I communed nightly with my "sweet secret." Because they express the connectedness between my body, my seed, and my God, I would frequently recite these verses from Psalm 139:

> *For you created my inmost being;*
> *you knit me together in my*
> *my mother's womb.*
> *I praise you because you made me*
> *in an amazing and wonderful way;*
> *your works are wonderful,*
> *I know that full well.*
> *My frame was not hidden from you*
> *when I was made in the secret place.*
> *When I was woven together in the*
> *depths in the earth,*
> *your eyes saw (and loved)*
> *my unformed body.*[1]

Over the tedious months of gestation, I strove to be both a nurturing mother-to-be and an attentive midwife. Monitoring my physical, emotional, and spiritual well-being, I wove the web of this mystical pregnancy with threads pulled out of the future instead of the past. The seed of my Re-Membered self beckoned me forward and focused my attention on the mature woman I was to become.

The Goddess Guide: Artemis

What is Artemis' genealogy?

Artemis was the first-born twin of Apollo, God of the Sun. Together, they have been called "the most glorious great-grandchildren of Gaia and Ouranos."[2] Her maternal grandparents were the Titan siblings, Koios and Phoebe. Kronos and Rhea were her paternal grandparents. Zeus was her father and Leto, a nature deity, was her mother.

What is Artemis' mythology?

The mythological origins of this major deity remain obscure and complex. It has been suggested that Artemis was probably an oriental goddess whose deeply rooted cult flourished in the rugged mountains of ancient Arcadia.[3] Though she was worshiped in many ways, Goddess of the Moon, Goddess of the Hunt, Goddess of Young Girls, Goddess who Slays, Moford and Lenardon state: "Artemis is predominantly a virgin goddess ... certain aspects of her character suggest that at some time she may have had fertility connections."[4] Guthrie suggests that in early Greek religion, Artemis was "an earth goddess associated with wildlife, fields, and childbirth."[5]

Prior to giving birth to her immortal twins, Leto had engendered the ire of Hera. As a product of her rage, Hera made certain that Leto would encounter extreme challenges, not only during her pregnancy but also at the time of her parturition. Because Hera's fits of jealousy were well known, Leto found it almost impossible to locate a place whose inhabitants were eager to help her in any way. Sensing her need and frustration, Zeus turned Leto into a she-wolf and, after twelve days in that disguise, she came to the wild and sparsely populated area of Delos (sometimes called Ortygia). Leto experienced an easy birth with Artemis. She was in hard labor for nine days and nights before Apollo was born, and Artemis served as her midwife.

One tale describes the young Artemis as an extremely precocious and self-directed child. Around the age of three she is said to have approached Zeus with these wishes: 1) to remain eternally youthful and virginal; 2) to claim the wilderness as her home; and, 3) to live in the company of nymphs and hounds. Graciously, Zeus acquiesced to all of his little daughter's desires. Moreover, Poseidon is said to have crafted her a silver bow and arrows, while Pan supplied her with pure-bred dogs.[6]

In addition to helping Leto birth Apollo, there are other myths that illustrate the close relationship between mother and daughter. It is said that after the giant Tityus attempted to rape Leto, Artemis, an unerring archer, took aim and "hit the bulls-eye." In another story, Niobe, the fertile, beautiful and boastful Queen of Thebes, verbally demeaned and insulted the twins' revered mother. In response, Apollo murdered Niobe' seven sons, and Artemis slew six of the Queen's seven daughters. Pleading for mercy and compassion, Niobe sought to protect her youngest child. Unrelenting, Artemis changed the mortal into stone and flung her high onto a mountain top where her tears continue to break through the hard rock.

There are various myths that depict the goddess' insistence on the inviolability of purity and chastity. One such story involves Acteon, an ardent hunter. Inadvertently, he comcs upon Artemis and her band of companions while they are bathing. The young man's gaze falls upon the goddess. In quick response to that violation, Artemis throws water in his face. At once, antlers begin to sprout from his forehead and he is changed into a stag. Acteon's own hounds soon turn on him, pursue him, and tear him to bits.

Another story of Artemis' revulsion of defilement is that of Callisto, one of the goddess' most beloved nymphs. One day, Zeus catches sight of Callisto in the woods. He decides that he must have her, and disguises himself as Artemis in order to realize his desire. Believing she is with her beloved goddess, Callisto engages in conversation. After a brief exchange of words, Zeus drops his disguise and forces himself upon her. Having kept considerable distance from Artemis for nine months, Callisto is forced to bathe in front of the goddess and the other nymphs. When Artemis discovers the truth about Callisto's condition, the goddess expels her forever from the band.

Like Hestia and Athena, Artemis never falls complete victim to the amorous powers of Aphrodite. As a trick, she promises to wed one of Poseidon' giant sons, Otus. He and his brother, Ephialtes, openly challenge the power of Zeus, and voice their desire to take Artemis and Hera as their brides. In response, an angry Zeus sends Ares, the god of war, to fight them. The giants grab Ares and, without much resistance, stuff him into a bronze jar. Apollo devises the plan whereby his sister's wiles result in the death of the giants as well as in Ares' freedom. Artemis deceives Otus by telling him she will marry him on the island of Naxos. A jealous Ephialtes agrees to accompany his brother. Upon seeing them, Artemis changes herself into a white stag. Both brothers attack the animal with their javelins, and end up killing each other.

Another myth involves Orion, an avid young hunter whom Artemis cares for deeply. Apollo is offended by the romantic feelings his sister expresses towards this mortal. He goads Artemis into shooting an arrow at a far-distant object that is floating in the sea. Apollo is aware that Orion is the object and that Artemis is sure to hit her target. Inadvertently, the goddess slays Orion. To allay her grief Artemis places Orion among the night stars and gifts him with Sirius, one of her favorite hunting dogs.

What makes Artemis a mythic mentor?

Artemis "seems to beckon from the future, to call me toward who I am now to become ... she inspires, she does not enchant."[7]

While becoming more familiar with the archetypal personality of Artemis, I was inspired by the wide range of her titles. Epithets such as Goddess of Chastity, Patroness of Young Girls, Goddess of the Hunt, Goddess of the Moon, Goddess of Childbirth, and Goddess of the Wilderness demonstrate the breadth of devotion to her in ancient times. Because of the depth and complexity of her identity, I chose this goddess to be my mentor and midwife. As I came to know more about Artemis, I had to admit that she had called to me continuously over several decades. It was only when I stood on the threshold of Stage IV and faced the midlife task of gestating my Adultwoman that I chose to turn and face her. At that point, I became receptive and responsive to her message: "Put yourself first!"

As Goddess of Chastity, Artemis models high expectations for her followers. Because many Greeks believed that a woman's virginity could be renewed,[8] Artemis insists that a woman renew her virginal sense of self during this stage of the Re-Membering rite. The concept of virginity within this context is purely symbolic. It carries with it the meaning of intactness or inviolability; that is, the idea of belonging to no one but oneself. As a mentor of hallowed purity and chastity, Artemis exemplifies femaleness in its virginal essence. The goddess is unwilling a) to disown her deep-seated feminine spirit, and b) to defile it in any way. Alone, she exudes self-confidence and self-direction.

Reinforcing her image as Goddess of Chastity, Artemis is also worshipped as Patroness of Young Girls. In Arcadia, evidence remains of an indigenous cult that flourished in her honor. At the age of nine or ten years, pubescent girls left their mothers and became Artemis' handmaidens. As part of their initiation, they donned saffron robes and wore bear skins over their shoulders. According to Christine Downing, the initiate, the goddess, and the bear "were considered to be one in nature and were called by the same name."[9] As a mentor, Artemis embodies the physical and psychological characteristics of her "she-bears." Dressed in a short tunic, bow and quiver slung over her shoulder, the goddess artistically resembles an androgynous youth. Not unlike my ten-year-old daughter, she exudes the attitude that "anything is possible and I, alone, can make it happen." Patriarchal beliefs and values have no hold on the goddess because Artemis "embodies a profound denial of the world of patriarchy."[10] Her thoughts and actions are chaste; that is, they are molded from within by her own curiosity, vitality, spontaneity, and ambition. Poised somewhere between childhood and womanhood, Artemis encourages followers to unearth and reflect upon what Emily Hancock calls their "root identity,"[11] that is, the seed of their femaleness which was either waylaid or shelved in favor of a culturally-defined feminine facade. Part of an initiate's task in Stage IV is to reconnect with that seed, the female soul, and nurture it as part of her prenatal care program.

As Goddess of the Hunt, Artemis embodies aspects of the female seed that are unbridled and instinctive. Representing "female being in its own essence,"[12] Artemis tenaciously hunts down and mercilessly destroys all that threatens to defile, demean, or destroy femaleness. Kerenyi calls her "the untamable virgin huntress."[13] Both Downing[14] and Clarissa Pinkola Estés[15] refer to her as "La Loba" or "The Wolf One." Estes also describes this archetypal respresentation of the primitive female psyche as "the Wild Woman."[16] As I learned more about Artemis, I was able to see those aspects of her personality depicted artistically. Portrayed as a beautiful, fearless, and self-assured huntress, the goddess frequently would be flanked by animals of the field or chase: the stag, wild boar, bear, hare, or wolf. Always, she looked strong, competent, and ready either to chase the quarry of her choosing or to be chased herself.

Under the aegis of Goddess of the Hunt, Artemis mentors her followers with straightforward teachings. As an unerring archer, she advises: "Focus on creating your identity from self-chosen beliefs, values, attitudes, and interests; then believe in your innate ability to 'hit the bullseye.'" As La Loba, Artemis whispers from a safe distance: "Breathe woman-soul into the mass of new identity that is developing within you. Become like the wolf—faithful, individualistic, strong, territorial, curious, protective, and nurturing." Finally, as Wild Woman, the divine huntress shrieks out from antiquity: "Don't be afraid of your instinctive nature. It will bring you success in the hunt for your authentic Self."

In my mind, Artemis' role as Goddess of the Moon further enhances her qualifications to mentor initiates through Stage IV of the Re-Membering rite. Symbolizing the cyclical nature of a woman's biological life dance, Artemis, the moon deity, casts light upon the events of birth, menarche, and menopause with her moon shadows. Because of her connection to the biological life cycle of women of all ages, Artemis is indeed, "the most woman-identified of all Greek goddesses."[17] Her "moonlight vision"[18] is another characteristic that initiates may well want to develop. At this time in the process of identity reformation, a woman's focus is drawn inward to the developing seed of her mature identity. Artemis' moonlight draws the initiate's eyes skyward, where they can feast upon a heavenly smorgasbord of stars. Like nectar and ambrosia, moonlight and starlight not only nourish the divine seed but also become its cosmic "grow" light.

After assisting Leto in the difficult labor and delivery of Apollo, Artemis shares the title of Goddess of Childbirth with Hera and Eileithyia. As a mentor in the Re-Membering rite, she is able to relate to her followers in the role of midwife. I have vivid recollections of living through both a literal and a figurative pregnancy. While carrying my daughter, I consistently deferred to the needs of others, giving scant attention to mine and my baby's. I was especially concerned that my "condition" should, in no way, impinge upon corporate goals, timelines, strategies, or relationships. Hindsight indicates clearly that many of the choices I made during that pregnant time either ignored or minimized the advice of my personal midwife. When I became pre-eclamptic for the second time, she gave me this warning: "Choose yourself or you'll injure your baby." Several years later, when I became psychologically pregnant with my Re-Membered self, I more readily accepted the advice of my mythic midwife: "Choose yourself and nurture your female seed!" Knowing Artemis to be a harsh judge of women, I monitored myself physically, mentally, emotionally, and spiritually so as not to fall short of her divine expectations.

Goddess of the Wilderness is the last epithet bestowed upon Artemis that influenced my choosing her as a mythic mentor. Literally the word "wilderness" means: "an empty or pathless area or region."[19] Women pregnant with the seeds of their Re-Membered selves stand at a crossroad somewhere between the two halves of their lives. Jean Shinoda Bolen speaks of Artemis' wilderness as "inner terrain." She goes on: " Women who follow Artemis into the wilderness discover themselves becoming more reflective ... dreams are more vivid than usual."[20] Like a matronly nymph in her company, over several months I followed Artemis into a wilderness space. During that time, I pursued my True Self in the untangible terrain of dreams. Frequently, I found myself wrestling with the hodgepodge overgrowth of surrealistic landscapes. In variants of one such dream, I would be the sole participant in a psychological Outward Bound adventure. After scaling a perpendicular cliff of rocks or thick vegetation, I would conquer the edge of the highest precipice. My body, dog-tired, would then be swept away into waterless waves of sweet-smelling grasses. Currents within that ocean of bending blades massaged me like the strong hands and fingers of an expert masseuse. Feeling reinvigorated, I would find myself standing in the foyer of a bone-white temple. From deep inside, female voices chanted unintelligible messages meant only for my ears. While I yearned to rush in and assume full membership in that esteemed sisterhood, I knew the door to the inner sanctum would remain locked to me until I deciphered the language and became fluent in it. Around that point, I would awaken to mixed-up memories of success and failure, happiness and sadness, wilderness and civilization, journeying and arriving.

What are some of Artemis's qualities?

A few essential features of Artemis's character are described in this Homeric Hymn to the Goddess:

> I sing about Artemis of the golden arrows, chaste virgin of the noisy hunt, who delights in her shafts and strikes down the stag, the very own sister of Apollo of the golden sword. She ranges over shady hills and windy heights, rejoicing in the chase as she draws her bow, made all of silver, and shoots her shafts of woe. The peaks of the lofty mountains tremble, the dark woods echo terribly to the shrieks of wild beasts, and both the earth and fish-filled sea are shaken. But she with dauntless heart looks everywhere to wreak destruction on the brood of animals. But when the huntress, who takes delight in her arrows, has had her fill of pleasure and cheered her heart, she unstrings her curved bow and makes her way to the great house of her brother, Apollo, in the rich land of Delphi, where she supervises the lovely dances of the Muses and the Graces. After she has hung up her unstrung bow and arrows, she takes first place and exquisitely attired leads the dance.[21]

Some qualities of Artemis' personality that her followers ought to emulate include her assertiveness, untamed spirit, androgynous nature, and leadership skills, as well as the mutually fulfilling relationship she enjoys with her mother.

Artemis knew what she wanted and needed, communicated those things clearly, then acted decisively to attain them. The goddess' disposition to speak out and act assertively on her own behalf became evident in early childhood. When very young, little Artemis expressed important wishes from her life's plan to Zeus. He not only granted all of them, but also helped her fulfill them. While in Stage IV, a woman in Artemis' service must practice a style of speaking and acting that reflects and reinforces aspects of her authentic self. Like La Loba, I had to breathe "woman soul" into the bones of that new identity blossoming within me by fleshing out my beliefs, my values, my needs, my wants, and my wishes.

Some writers in feminine psychology and spirituality might call Artemis' untamed spirit "the female soul." To me, her wild nature is more akin to the spark that both ignites and illumines her centerpoint or core. When talking about the instinctive aspect of the Wild Woman archetype, Clarissa Pinkola Estés uses various descriptors: "the incubator of raw ideas, the glowing cell, the loyal heart, maker of cycles, the mind which thinks us, the source of the feminine."[22] At midlife, the initiate needs to nourish her embryonic sense of mature self with qualities that are second-nature to her untamed goddess guide. A Re-Membering woman must resurrect and fine-tune her instinctive abilities to sense, track, run, hide, wait, camouflage, entice, aim at, and hit her chosen target.

Artemis has also been described as being androgynous. As such, she displays characteristics that are both feminine and masculine. It is essential that her followers, at this stage in re-birthing their mature identity, assess the degree of androgyny within their former sense of self. I discovered, for example, that as I quested for the Holy Grail of success during the first half of my life, I moved like one of Artemis' well-aimed arrows toward its clearly defined target. Consciously and unconsciously, I focused on and nurtured primarily masculine traits within myself. Those seemed to reflect most accurately aspects of our culturally-based definition of that concept: linearity, objectivity, autonomy, independence, logical thinking, achievement, and aggression. During my period of gestation, I had to renegotiate the direction of the path I cleared through that untamed territory. I found myself moving spirally backward and rediscovering the long-empty chambers that held the seeds of my feminine nature: feelings, intuition, healing, listening, sexuality, creativity, nurturance, negotiation, relationship, and spirituality. Taking the lead from my androgynous mentor, I visualized the Authentic Adultwoman, developing within my intrapsychic womb, to be in absolute balance.

Artemis' association with her nymph-companions bespeaks her fitness to lead. When contemplating nuances of the goddess' leadership style, I was struck by the level of her expertise. I felt inspired both to search for and to cultivate within myself some of these traits: fearlessness, single-mindedness, loyalty, decisiveness, integrity, consistency, trustworthiness, and self-sufficiency. From somewhere in the wild terrain of becoming, Artemis challenged me "to take up the lead" in my maneuvering into midlife.

Artemis and Leto avoided experiencing the "mother/daughter split,"[23] a major stage in Maureen Murdock's model of the heroine's journey towards wholeness. She described that psychological gash as separating a young woman's emerging identity from her feminine nature thus causing her to deny or degrade aspects of her own wonderful womanhood. The split seems to be inflicted some time during adolescence, from two separate directions: internally, by the "she-bear" herself, and externally, by her mother. Around the time my breasts began budding, I intuited the paradoxical nature of motherhood within the context of a patriarchal society: although revered, it was an institution that carried little prestige and even less power. Unconsciously, I decided that I wanted to end up being more successful than moms generally seemed to be. Simultaneously, my mother started to have difficulties dealing with my need to differentiate myself from her. As a result of that and other factors, I turned my head away from my innate feminine attributes, bought into the culturally-accepted myths concerning femininity, then for several years focused all of my unbalanced energy on "really making it" in a man's world.

Since Artemis vehemently rejected the assumptions and values inherent in a patriarchal culture, and Leto was secure enough in herself to accept unconditionally her divine offspring, these two women enjoyed an uninterrupted relationship of mutual interdependence and respectful support. Because Stage IV revolves around the mystery of becoming mother to one's sense of mature self, it is the time in a woman's development when she needs to lance the wound of self-rejection inflicted by "the mother/daughter split," cleanse it with the blessed ointments of forgiveness and self-love, then allow it to heal fully from within. When I was struggling to remove the invisible scar left in my mind and heart by "the split," I experienced feelings that ranged from pity and mild resentment to blatant rage. For months, I ranted about my perception of mom as having been self-centered, jealous, angry, fearful, controlling, and rigid. Artemis' relationship with Leto helped me not only rediscover the divine connection that exists between mother and daughter, but also to appreciate and heal the human one. By so doing, I facilitated the task that I had to master at this point in my rite of passage: to gestate my Re-Membered sense of identity.

Stage IV Tasks and Strategies

The primary task the initiate needs to master in Stage IV focuses on the concept of generativity; that is, gestating aspects of her Re-Membered self by reconnecting with her feminine nature. At the beginning of this stage, you have already passed several grueling tests on your path of personal transformation: acknowledging and grieving historical wounds, dissecting an ego-generated sense of self, letting go of limiting or even destructive aspects of that former identity, and not only facing into your personal demons but also embracing them. To a great extent, you have made peace with your past. Now, you need to focus on designing a future that allows you to embrace yourself as a mature woman. Below are some ideas that will enhance your abilities to function as a competent yet compassionate creatrix:

- Nurture an embryonic sense of self that is vital and authentic by identifying beliefs, values, interests, and needs reflective of a "real you."
- Sculpt balance into your Re-Membering consciousness by examining beliefs and behaviors that are gender-based. Think about those traits that make you feel comfortable/uncomfortable as well as balanced/unbalanced. Are you missing essential traits that are either masculine or feminine? Plan ways in which you can either capitalize on those traits that already are evident or develop those that are weak or absent.
- Get into your creatrix role by trying out something new. Dare to be different by choosing to accept the challenges engendered through risk-taking and change. Create a new image for yourself by changing your hair style or make-up, explore a new interest, practice the gifts of creativity, spontaneity, and innovation at home as well as at work.
- Live in the present but focus on the future. Like your mythic mentor, focus on realistic goal-setting by clearly defining your target and taking careful aim. By so doing, you become a proactive participant in the hunt for your Re-Membered self. The topic of goal-setting is featured in many seminars, workshops, and published self-help texts.
- Create an emotionally enriching environment for your gestating identity. Feed with affirmative thoughts the embryonic vision you hold of your True Self. Acknowledge that the

growth and development of your Adultwoman will be affected by a variety of internal and external stressors, including thoughts, behaviors, and relationships.

- Heal to the best of your ability any emotional wounds that exist between yourself and your mother. Read about mother/daughter relationships, talk to other women, try to smooth out infractions through the gift of forgiveness. It may, however, be impossible for you to communicate with your mother and maintain your sense of integrity. If that is the case, it is essential that you accept responsibility for emancipating yourself from her identity, definitions, expectations, and approval.
- Expand your relationships with women in order to create a support network. You may wish to join a book club, development group, prayer circle, or professional organization.
- Think about attitudes you have embraced concerning the archetypal image of the Wild Woman. To what extent have you connected with this instinctive part of yourself? Have you any evidence that she exists within you? How does she look, act, and make you feel? Consider the impact she has on your relationships.
- Find someone with whom you can connect intimately. This relationship need NOT be sexual in nature; however, it is important that you be able to relate deeply to another individual. You may choose to call this person spouse, partner, friend, mentor, or counselor.
- Allocate time to engage in daydreaming and wish-making. Enjoy those periods because they will help you focus more on becoming and less on doing.
- Keep in mind that the Re-Membering rite is simultaneously evolutionary and involutionary. Like the Dromenon, the

path through this developmental process is in the form of a spiral. As such, it embodies the paradox that to expand outward one must move inward.

✧ Enthusiastically prepare for the birth of your Re-Membered self.

Stage IV's Major Obstacles

"Midlifers" in Stage IV have to be aware of two factors that could impede their progress. These are their impatience and a denial of their vulnerability.

As I approached the end of Stage IV, I recall feeling more energized and enthusiastic than I had felt in almost two years. Thinking about the future and my role in it proved to be an exciting pastime. Instead of feeling washed-over in greyish tones, my life's canvas now would be spattered intermittently with passionate reds, brilliant yellows, and hope-filled greens. I yearned to bathe myself in such vibrance on a more regular basis—it felt so good! Frequently, I became impatient with myself and with how long my interapsychic pregnancy was lasting. "When would my new identity emerge?" was a question that stalked me. From time to time, I became angry, fatigued, and frustrated at feeling I had to assume a "holding pattern" on life. When I turned those negative feelings inward, my life's bright colors would run together in dark streams of depression. I would become immobile. In time, I came to see impatience as a "red flag" symbolizing lingering attachments to my former self and its desire to control external and internal circumstances.

For months, a second factor kept me stuck in Stage IV like psychological quicksand. I had to acknowledge and accept the fact that to be human is to be vulnerable. Part of me still expected my Adultwoman to be "divinely extraordinary"; that is, consistently unassailable, compassionate, logical, in control, decisive, competent, and unemotional. Not until I gave my Re-Membering self permission to be wounded did my "divinely ordinary"[24] identity reposition herself and begin the birthing process.

A Reflective Exercise

These exercises are designed to help you conceive and nurture the seed of your Re-Membered identity—that sense of self you will don during the second half of your life. Before you begin, allow your body, mind, and heart to become relaxed and receptive. Pay close attention to your breathing. Think about the miracle embodied in the mystery of "immaculate conception." It is your responsibility, alone, to assume the roles of both mother and midwife. As before, I strongly suggest that you journal your responses, and that you complete them at your leisure. It is impossible to hasten the due date of this pregnancy. At some point in the future, you may decide to discuss insights from your journal with a supportive companion.

a) Find a photograph of yourself around the age of nine or ten years. If you are unable to resurrect such a picture, create one in your mind using your imagination. Study the way you look, feel, think, and act. If you choose, sketch this budding "she-bear" that still resides within you. Dialogue with her. Here is a way you might begin your conversation:

   Hello, ______________________ (use the name or nickname to which you responded at that age). What things would you like to say to me? What are your likes/dislikes? Does anything about me scare you? Do you have any special dreams about yourself? What do you want to be when you grow up? What makes you unique?

b) Brainstorm traits that are both masculine and feminine. Put an "X" next to those you perceive as being masculine and an "O" in front of those that seem feminine. Circle all of those that you see in yourself. How balanced do they seem to be within your personality? Do you need to develop traits in either gender category? Have any of these traits been a source of pride, pleasure, or pain to you?

c) Close your eyes and create an image in your mind of your Adultwoman identity. Visualize her incubating deep within the center of your being. Study her from different angles—her physical characteristics, needs, interests, values, accomplishments, beliefs, desires, masculine/feminine traits, gifts, vulnerabilities, life purpose, and so on. How do you feel about bringing this developing entity to term?

d) Bond with your Re-Membering self by talking to her in "angel whispers," affirmations about her that answer this question: "What love-filled or self-accepting messages would you communicate to an infant?" Brainstorm your "whispers" on paper because you may want to tape record them later. Below are a few examples:

   You are lovable. You are capable.

   You deserve pleasure. You have many gifts.

   You need not be afraid. You can trust me.

   You attract loving relationships.

e) Think about the relationship that has developed between you and your mother over time. List characteristics that you admire/detest in her. Especially study those traits that continue to touch raw nerves in you. What are they? Do you see the same traits in yourself? Have you emancipated fully from your mother? What is her legacy to you in terms of physical characteristics, temperament, and so on? What have you learned about yourself as a result of your relationship with her? How has your relationship been a source of pleasure, pain, growth, or stagnation? If you are emotionally estranged from your mother, is there any way forgiveness of her and yourself might heal that wound?

f) Artemis is recognized as an accomplished archer. As an archetypal mentor, she can help women set and attain goals. In this exercise, using the form below, focus on stipulating two goals in each area that are meaningful as well as realistic.

Goal	**Time frame**	**Obstacles**
Personal		
Professional		
Familial		
Communal		
Social		

g) Think about the "Wild Woman" part of your identity. On paper, brainstorm her characteristics. How does she look, feel, behave? What do you admire, dislike, or fear in her? How has she manifested herself in your life? What role does she play in your Re-Membering rite of passage?

h) Pay close attention to your dreams. Write them down, title and study them. Have any included journeys, wild terrain, chases, births?

i) Plan and give a shower in anticipation of your new arrival. Who will you invite? Who will you certainly not invite? What gifts might you anticipate receiving? Buy her a special gift and create a card in honor of the occasion.

Ritual for Stage IV: Breathing Woman-Soul into Your Seed

To help you bring closure to Stage IV, this ritual requires that you call forth the highly creative and generative parts of yourself. Paula Hardin states: "the path of generativity helps us avoid the dangers of self-absorption and stagnation because we learn to live in new ways that expand our horizons."[25] The task at midlife is to expand your consciousness into middle age and beyond. Maintaining the same identity that served you during the first half of your life will surely result in stagnancy. Thus far, yours has been a generative metamorphosis. You have readdressed early losses, released destructive or limiting parts of your identity, reclaimed your psychological maidenhood, and reconnected with your feminine life-force. At this point in the process, you must continue your expansion by redefining your self-image to include this triune: midwife, mother, and incubating seed of Adultwoman.

Before you begin this ritual, you will want to arrange your altar or sacred space. Beautify it with flowers, plants, and adornments of different colors. Arrange three candles, one white for innocence, one red for life, and one green for hope-filled growth. If you have been pregnant, you may choose to place a photograph of yourself in that condition on your altar. If you have never been pregnant or have experienced the loss of a baby through miscarriage or abortion, find a token that symbolizes either pregnancy or motherhood to you and place it on your sacred space. Finally, assemble these materials if you decide to follow the ritual as outlined below: a fist-sized ball of modeling clay, a packet of small seeds, and your list of "angel whispers."

Standing in front of the altar, close your eyes. Take note of how the eyelids follow your silent command. Next, focus on your breathing. With each inhalation, give your imagination permission to concentrate on images and thoughts of being pregnant. Visualize the unbroken umbilicus deep within you that connects your Re-Membering sense of self to its feminine source. Next, turn slowly and stop momentarily facing each direction. Invite mothers of the east, south, west, and north to be present with you and happy for you.

Open your eyes and light the green candle. Focus your attention on the flame until you feel its blossom opening within you. Place your palms over your navel as you repeat the following thought:

SEED THOUGHT:
I am a birthing vessel
Pregnant with a precious treasure
called (name).

Pick up the clay and knead it until it is soft and pliable. Reverently, sculpt it into a female figure or a symbol that represents your embryonic Adultwoman. When your sculpting is complete, hold it in your hand. As you look at it, recite several of your "angel whispers."

Still holding your clay figure, invoke your mentor's presence with these thoughts:

Invocations

Artemis, embue her with your confidence.

Artemis, teach her self-sufficiency.

Artemis, lead her in the hunt for authenticity.

Artemis, direct her towards inner balance.

Artemis, accept her as your companion.

Artemis, help her embrace her instinctive nature.

Artemis, guide her across this wilderness terrain.

Artemis, impart to her your reverence for womanhood.

Artemis, attend her birth as midwife.

Count out the number of seeds that represent positive traits you wish to bestow upon your developing identity. Press each seed, one by one, into the clay accompanied by this thought: I gift you with the seed of wisdom (confidence, self-love, compassion, and so on). When you have "seeded" your new self, breathe woman-soul into her three times, then, light the white and red candles. Enjoy the sanctity of silence as you watch the flames dance in celebration. After a time, hum or sing your favorite lullaby to your gestating sense of self.

Close your ritual with a prayer, song, or gesture of your choice. Finally, you may choose to journal about thoughts and feelings you had before, during, and following this ritual.

SUMMARY

STAGE IV: THE GESTATION

NATURE GUIDE
An Acorn

MYTHIC MENTOR
Artemis

MENTOR QUALITIES
Virginal
Goal-oriented
Comfortable with wilderness
Androgynous
Assertive
Ability to lead, decisive, confident
Closely connected to women
Positive relationship with mother

PRIMARY TASK
To gestate aspects of Re-Membered identity.

PRIMARY STRATEGIES
Become self-observant
Try new things
Network with peers
Identify values, beliefs, interests
Explore mother-daughter split
Daydream
Know your Wild Woman
Nurture yourself
Prepare for rebirth

MAJOR OBSTACLE(S)
Impatience
Denial of Vulnerability

RITUAL FOCUS
Creativity

WHOM MIGHT YOU ENCOUNTER?
Your Wild Woman

A woman gives birth to herself
as a divine androgynous being,
autonomous,
and in a state of perfection ...
She is whole.

Maureen Murdock
The Heroine's Journey

STAGE FIVE: THE RE-BIRTH

NATURE GUIDE: A BUTTERFLY

Riding an invisible zephyr around Lake Como, this scaly-winged guide lighted upon a clover blossom that was within stretching distance of my big toe. With wings resting vertically over its slender body, my transient teacher eagerly drank her host's nectar, then seemed to point her club-tipped antennae in my direction. For a moment, I felt that all of the thousand lenses encased in her enormous eyes were riveted upon me. Responding to the butterfly's unspoken mandate, I picked up my journal and began to jot down thoughts:

"You, my two-legged sister, resemble me in ways that you probably have never imagined. First, my specialized sense of vision distinguishes shadowy wing-like structures within the energy field that surrounds you. Such appendages, although invisible to your human eye, speak to me of your heavenly or divine lineage and symbolize your innate entitlement to the gift of freedom.

"A second way in which you and I are similar is in terms of the journey we take as we move toward maturity. Butterflies pass through four distinct stages of development: egg, larva or caterpillar, pupa, and adult. The process, called metamorphosis, entails dramatic changes in our physical structure between conception and full adulthood. While in utero, human creatures experience this striking metamorphic transfiguration: from zygote, to embryo, to fetus, to infant. I believe that both the exterior and interior structures of human beings continue to metamorphose after their emergence into this earth-bound world. Like me, you experience subsequent 'births' which are most visible at adolescence and midlife.

"Somewhere during my pre-adult stage of development, I outgrew my exoskeleton four or five times. It appears to me that human beings 'molt' too. As a caterpillar, my primary task was to eat a great deal of food in order to provide the energy needed for my continued growth. Very simply, my body grew but my skin stayed the same size. When it became too tight, it split down the center of my back and I crawled out of it. Don't you think a similar thing happens, metaphorically of course, to adults of your species? For three decades or more, you feed your sense of self on cultural expectations, family traditions, and institutional injunctions. That way, you obtain the energy necessary to make adulthood happen. Next, between the years of thirty-five and forty-five, you begin to feel cramped inside the 'skin' or identity that served you so well during the first half of your life. With inadequate understanding and preparation, you begin to experience the multiple sheddings that are characteristic of what you call midlife transition.

"The most traumatic stage of my metamorphosis was when I became a pupa. I had to prepare well in advance for this period in my life. First, I found a physical place where I was able to feel safe. Next, I deposited a sticky liquid on a twig growing near the top of a tall tree. That liquid quickly hardened into a silklike pad. The next step was especially scary for me. The last layer of my caterpillar skin split open near my head. I emerged a pupa. Instinct told me to attach my soft body to the silky pad, using the claw-like structures that were on my underside. That move spelled d-a-n-g-e-r because, if I missed the target, I would fall to the ground. Luckily for me, I executed this maneuver without a hitch. As soon as I felt secure, a hard shell or chrysalis began to form all around my body. It seemed as if I remained motionless in that dark pod forever. Finally, the shell broke open and, when I stretched, wings and a brand new body emerged. I think human beings go through a similar period of darkness during their adult development. Yours may be more difficult to carry out, though, because you can neither build a silken pad around yourself nor 'hang out' for as long as you need to re-form yourself into a mature adult.

"The final aspect of the way in which I see similarities between you and me is the brevity of our lives on earth. With good fortune, mine may add up to several weeks and you may count yours in decades. Nonetheless, in contrast to some of our relatives in the plant or mineral kingdoms, life for us can be over in the blink of an eye.

"Well, my two-legged cousin, did you know that the ancient Greeks believed that, after death, the soul left the body in the form of a butterfly? What an honor! In fact, their symbol for the soul was a butterfly-winged girl called Psyche. Like her, your feminine soul is winged. Today, Mother Nature sent me to you with this message: Your time, daughter, has come. The birthing hour is at hand. Allow your Re-Membered self to emerge. Greet your Adultwoman with love. Encourage her to spread her wings, then fly with her into the future."

When the stream of thought stopped, the butterfly flew away. As I watched her graceful air-borne dance, I sent her thoughts of gratitude. After she had left my sacred space, I closed my eyes and entered the image of my milky-white messenger into my long-term memory. Next, I began to search my mental data base for key words and ideas that the butterfly had just used. "Divine lineage," "metamorphic transfiguration," "molt," "chrysalis," and, "birthing hour" came quickly to mind.

It thrilled me to envision my feminine soul and my female body with angelic appendages. Through faith, I had long accepted this theory of possibility: my divine or spiritual roots were anchored securely in heavenly realms, and, when my soul decided to clothe itself in a human robe, it winged its way downward on an involutionary path toward planet earth. Somehow, my butterfly guide had validated that piece of intuitive wisdom.

Like two strong hands with long groping fingers, the words "metamorphic transfiguration" reached out and grabbed me. Could it be that the striking changes occurring within my body, mind, and heart were exalting, glorifying, or spiritual in nature? I knew that the identity to which I was about to give birth, my Re-Membered Self, would somehow reflect supernatural influences. By rediscovering the eternal connection to her ancient heritage and divine feminine soul, my Adultwoman would be able to be authentic, feel whole, act self-assured, live in balance, and love unconditionally. Indeed, I was being transfigured.

At first, when I thought of myself as a creature who periodically molted, I felt uncomfortable. To my mind, "molt" was a four-letter word ascribed to members of my extended family that wore feathers, fur, horns, or scales. Upon reflection, I came to understand how my Re-Membering rite of passage was really about mid-life molting in several dimensions. Physically, I had begun to cast off remnants of a more youthful me: natural auburn highlights, nipped-in waistline, cellulite-free "tush," enviable muscle tone, bionic energy, and predictable periods. Upon closer and more candid scrutiny, I felt forced to admit that I was also shedding mentally and emotionally. Over the past several years, I had let go of a mind-set that had manufactured and maintained a false sense of identity. I conferred and carried out the death sentence on three destructive aspects of my personality—Helpless Victim, Perfect Mom, and Masterful Male. Concerning my feeling life, I realized that I had spent a great deal of time during the past several months "peeling onions." The core of my affective nature had been covered over with thick juicy layers of unexpressed emotion. I found the paper-thin skin on the outside easy to remove, but began to anguish when I had to cut deeper and penetrate layers of fear, pain, and rage. Finally, I threw off a blanket of male mistrust that had insulated me from relationships and isolated me from intimacy for far too many years.

When my winged cousin described her chrysalis as a dark pod, I knew exactly what she meant. I named my chrysalis "Depression." While encased in the darkness of my mind's own making, I felt my body fall limp, my heart split open, and my spirit shatter. I hung suspended in that paradoxical pod month after month. Within it, reality became illusion, a tomb became a womb, darkness became light, sorrow become joy, and hatred became love. Did my depressive encasement facilitate or impede my maturation? Did it provide transcendent shelter for a burned-out Superwoman? Did I share the darkness with benefic or malevolent spirits? In her autobiography, Ann Keiffer spoke of depression as the Dark Angel, and described the unexpected gifts presented to her by this winged messenger.[1] How effortlessly my nature guide had reframed the perception I had of my depression. With a flutter of her wings, she managed to transform a well of despair into a wellspring of creativity and power.

Birthing hour. What did that mean exactly? Like magnets, the words pulled my awareness back in time to the day my daughter was born. I recall the timid twinges of early labor, the rhythms of focused breathing, the pleasure-filled pain of pushing, and the ecstacy of counting tiny fingers and toes. My parthenogenic pregnancy at midlife had been long and difficult. I was eager for the onset of labor and anxious to embrace the body, mind, and spirit of my Adultwoman. Within the security of my sacred space, I decided to make myself comfortable on Mother Nature's birthing bed. I breathed deeply and awaited the emergence of my Re-Membered identity.

The Goddess Guide: Ariadne

What is Ariadne's genealogy?

Known as Mistress of the Labyrinth, Ariadne was one of five offspring sired by Minos, King of Crete, and Pasiphae, a daughter of Helios, the sun-god. While Phaedra was her only sister, Hippolytus, Androgeos, and the monstrous Minotaur were her brothers.

What is Ariadne's mythology?

According to Kerenyi, Ariadne means "holy" or "pure," and is the superlative form of Hagne, Queen of the Underworld.[2] Such an association suggests evidence of a strong conne\'tion between her and Persephone, Demeter's daughter, who is abducted and raped by Hades, god of the Underworld.

Worshiped also as The Untouched One, Great Mother, and the Potent One,[3] Ariadne appears to have been far more powerful than a mere mortal who attained immortality as a result of her marriage to the Olympian god, Dionysos. Some scholars suggest that she was actually an ancient prepatriarchal goddess who became divested of her divine nature by becoming human. Morford and Lenardon state "Ariadne is originally a divine person, perhaps another form of Aphrodite."[4]

The mythological tales surrounding Ariadne are varied. The version that follows is a paraphrase from Kerenyi's work and appears in *Female Authority*[5]:

> Ariadne is the daughter of Minos and Queen Pasiphae. Pasiphae is sometimes called the daughter of the moon, sometimes of the sun. Pasiphae mated with a great white bull in a fit of rage, to produce the monstrous Minotaur, the brother of Ariadne.
>
> The Minotaur plagued the people of Crete for many years, requiring sacrifices of Athenian youths and maidens every nine years. Finally, the hero, Theseus comes to Crete from Athens with a special mission to slay this monster and save the people of Crete.

One of the best known versions of the labyrinthine myth has Theseus coming to Crete to save fourteen children of Athenian nobility from being sacrificed to the Minotaur. Falling in love with "her hero," Ariadne agrees to help him enter the labyrinth, kill her brother, and leave the maze without being harmed. To accomplish the task, the infatuated girl agrees to stand at the entrance of the labyrinth holding on to a thread that will allow Theseus to retrace his steps successfully. After doing that, she and Theseus leave Crete, along with the Athenian children and her sister, Phaedra. As they journey back to Athens, the ship stops at the island of Naxos. There, as a result of Artemis' punishment for eloping with Theseus and being unfaithful to her brother, Theseus abandons his helpmate and goes on to marry her sister. In one tale, Ariadne awakens from a deep sleep, realizes her plight, and grieves uncontrollably. Seeing her in that condition, Dionysos emerges from the clouds and takes her to be his only wife.

Another version has Ariadne betrothed to Dionysos prior to the arrival of Theseus. The god has given the girl a wreath of lights that was a gift to him from the goddess, Aphrodite. Ariadne uses the illuminated wreath to lead Theseus out of the labyrinth. In a dream, the hero is told that he will never marry Ariadne because she is already betrothed to Dionysos. When the god rescues the forlorn heroine on Naxos, he takes the wreath from her forehead and places it in the heavens where it can be seen today as the constellation, Corona.

There are several stories concerning Ariadne's death. One has her dying of grief. Another has her committing suicide on the Island of Naxos. Yet a third has her being killed just prior to giving birth. Artemis takes Ariadne's life as punishment for her infidelity to Dionysos. In that last version, Ariadne is carrying his child. She and the unborn child enter the realm of the dead where she gives birth.[6]

What makes Ariadne a mythic mentor?

Stage V culminates with an initiate making an active choice to birth her Re-Membered sense of self. That image, spiritual or divine in nature, bears the title of Authentic Adultwoman. To ease her movement through this stage, the initiate can look to Ariadne for knowlege and support. As mentor, this guardian of the serpentine path empowers her followers to enter the spiral maze, accompanies them back into its center, and leads them out safely.

When I moved into Stage V, I claimed Ariadne as my mentor for specific reasons: 1) she represented an "anima" figure; 2) she experienced both betrayal and abandonment; 3) she married Dionysos, an Olympian acclaimed for his feminine traits; 4) she gave birth to a divine child while in the Underworld; and, 5) she evolved from immortal goddess to mortal woman, and back to an immortal deity.

Ariadne offers a special lesson to contemporary women because she is an anima or "soul-making"[7] figure. In Kerenyi's opinion, The Mistress of the Labyrinth represents "the archetypal reality of bestower of soul, of what makes a living creature an individual."[8] Downing further describes this anima aspect of Ariadne as "soul in the sense of what is at the center of the labyrinth, what is at the center of the self."[9] It is especially important that Superwomen look to Ariadne as their role model during this rebirthing stage of development called midlife. While a member of that highly esteemed "cult," I raced along a labyrinthine track that pulled me farther and farther away from my feminine soul. As I focused upon the Re-Membered woman that was about to emerge from deep within my psyche, I asked Ariadne to guide me back to her, bestow soul upon her, and then lead us both safely out of the midlife maze.

As a result of helping Theseus find his soul deep in the center of the labyrinth, Ariadne becomes a mythic mentor with first-hand knowledge of betrayal and abandonment. She places her trust in a mortal hero and empowers him to penetrate the maze and kill her brother, the Minotaur. Although Theseus symbolizes the heroic dimension of masculinity as a patriarchical figure, he violates Ariadne's trust by leaving her alone on a deserted island, and returns victorious to Athens. Women, especially Superwomen, know all too well how it feels to be betrayed and abandoned by anthrocentric or male-defined values, beliefs, and institutions. With their numbers increasing almost exponentially, Ariadne's followers are experiencing betrayal of their marriage vows, abandonment by their spouses, and burnout in their careers. Somewhere during development, my sense of identity seemed to get mixed up when I began to sculpt it around a male-oriented model of success. When I began to review Act I of my life in my early forties, I felt betrayed by my dreams and abandoned by the patriarchal system. Downing, however, exonerates Theseus of any conscious act of cruel desertion by having him grieve his loss and by implying that Ariadne had to be left alone as a necessary prelude to her coming into contact with the divine Dionysos.[10]

Ariadne's relationship to Dionysos is key to understanding her role as mythic mentor in Stage V. Like Ariadne, Dionysos is psychologically androgenous. Frequently acknowledged as the womanly one, Dionysos was born from Zeus' thigh and raised as a girl by the maenads. He represents a complex god who balances both masculine sexuality and feminine soul. Dionysos represents "the lover of women who have their center in themselves, who are not defined by their relationships with literal men."[11] As Dionysos' chosen one, Ariadne must also reflect an inner balance between her sensuality and her soul. In experiencing abandonment and death, Ariadne discovers that blessed balance. Thereafter, she merges with her divine essence, and becomes transformed into a goddess. For decades, Superwomen have worshipped the divine masculine perspective that has permeated our culture and permutated our minds. As "The Potent One,"[12] Ariadne helps the initiate reactivate a sense of ancient power and divine heritage by reconnecting with the Dionysian past of herself, the aspect I call the Merciful Male. Also, she guides the initiate in balancing the masculine and feminine aspects of her Re-Membered image.

Another reason why Ariadne is the appropriate mentor for Stage V is the intimate relationship she weaves between love, death, and birth. In order to transcend human love and to realize her own immortality, she has to become the spouse of Dionysos. Prior to that transfiguring event, however, the mortal girl's death is arranged by her betrothed through the intercession of Artemis. Various mythic traditions describe Ariadne as dying in different ways. In addition to divine intervention, they include death by grief, suicide, and childbirth. Downing summarizes the last version in which both Ariadne and her unborn child by Dionysos die. While in the realm of the dead, Ariadne gives birth to a unique new soul; the offspring of her divinely masculine and sacred feminine self.[13] At this stage of the rite of passage, Ariadne awaits individual followers at the entrance of a labyrinthine birthing room. As each one crosses the threshold, the goddess assures her of safe entry and exit by having her hold onto the threads of love, death, and birth. Having been empowered by Ariadne to follow the spiral path back to her center or feminine soul, the initiate realizes that her former sense of self had to die in order for her to give birth to a divinely conceived identity.

Finally, I believe that Ariadne's metamorphic circle dance from deity to mortal back to deity reflects the mystical route that all of her followers experience at midlife. One ancient Cretan version of Ariadne's mythology suggests that during the earliest of matriarchical times, she was "a goddess complete in herself."[14] When androcentrism or male-domination emerged as the cultural norm, goddess figures were divested of their power through dissection into more manageable divine forms or through humanization. Through Ariadne's mentoring, I came to accept the belief that my authentic identity was a) divinely inspired and spiritual in nature; b) encased temporarily in a human vessel; c) connected to my feminine nature; and, d) buried deep beneath a false sense of self. The Re-Birthing Stage of the transformation process was the time in which my true identity emerged Re-Membered.

What are some of Ariadne's qualities?

As the initiate prepares to birth her Re-Membered self in the form of a mature woman, she would do well to emulate a few of Ariadne's qualities. Some of the most obvious are her abilities to mediate, to empower others, to do service, and to be compassionate and self-initiating.

The thread she holds for Theseus symbolizes Ariadne's ability to interpose herself successfully between two opposing parties or ideas. She represents, for example, a mythic intermediary who brings a sense of reconciliation between mortality and immortality, masculinity and femininity, birth and death, matriarchy and patriarchy, the body and the soul. A woman who is rebirthing the virginal identity of Re-Membered self must actively mediate between two specific stages of her development, young adulthood and middle age. Also, she has to be able to reconcile differences between the past and present, the real and the unreal.

The need to be more like Ariadne comes when a woman must learn to empower others. That quality or gift comes almost instinctively to women. The art of empowering refers to the ability to enable another person to behave in a certain way or to carry out a specific act. The initiate in Stage V is confronted with the task of empowering her Re-Membered sense of self to enter the labyrinthine birth canal of the mind, reconnect with the feminine soul that dwells deep within the heart, and emerge an alert, balanced, and confident woman.

In helping Theseus slay her brother, Ariadne demonstrates the admirable quality of doing service to others. The Minotaur, a product of their mother's rageful mating with a great white bull, plagues the people of Crete, devours those who reach the center of its labyrinthine dwelling, and demands human flesh for sustenance. Every ninth year, he consumes fourteen Athenian youngsters: seven boys and seven girls. Acknowledging the need to eliminate this source of evil, Ariadne serves the common good by helping to bring about his death.

Unlike Persephone, who was abducted to the Underworld by Hades, Ariadne's entry into the labyrinth of her inner world was self-generated. Responding to intuitive urges, the mortal girl acted out of her own value system. The consequences for taking such risks were growth-producing; she reconnected with forgotten features of her feminine psyche, recognized her soul's bisexual nature, and reemerged whole and free.

Stage V Tasks and Strategies

My passage into Stage V was heralded by a marked surge in energy and a most welcome sense of anticipation. Those two gifts softened the more painful memories I had of birthing's "downside." I felt ready, willing, and able for the work that was ahead of me.

The task on which I had to focus was to give birth to and embrace my revirginated and Re-Membered sense of identity, my Authentic Adultwoman. I discovered that there were specific ways I could ready myself for her birth. Many of those strategies revolved around issues of trust, responsibility, support, solitude, and spirituality. I have described them below:

- Facilitate the birthing process by reconnecting with nature. Assemble especially meaningful guides and allies that have come to you from nature's realm. Many Native American traditions refer to such an item as a Medicine Bundle. I called mine a Re-Birthing Bundle. On a daily basis, I asked those special friends to help me experience an uncomplicated birth.

- Assess the level of trust you have in men, your male psyche, and our patriarchical society. While scores of women have valid reasons for no longer placing absolute faith in the male "other," it is imperative that cynicism not overtake discernment.

- Assume responsibility for your thoughts, words, and actions. You began doing this prior to Stage V, but now personal accountability includes letting go of two very human tendencies: projecting blame on others and failing to forgive them.

- Locate and use peer support as you move through your rebirthing process. Choose those women who have moved beyond Stage III in their own midlife rite of passage.

- Simplify things. An infant requires that mom be "on call" around-the-clock. While your Authentic Adultwoman will be far less demanding, she will need you to build time into your schedule to accommodate her needs and wants. Simplification will bring more balance and nurturance into Act II of your life.

- Honor the wisdom of sitting in solitude prior to and after the emergence of your Re-Membered Self. A woman's sense of harmonious union is stabilized by quieting her mind. The uncomfortable feeling of fragmentation dissipates and wholeness takes hold of the heart.

- ✧ Nurture your Adultwoman. Even though your Re-Membered identity is rooted deep within the soul, she needs to be shown in word and deed that she is loved, heard, and valued.
- ✧ Celebrate the spiritual essence of your transformed identity. If "spirituality is the spilling out of an inner reality,"[15] your Re-Membered identity represents a creative self-portrait of that inner world in you which is closest to God.

Stage V's Major Obstacles

When reading research about aging (and listening to my intuition), I hear a strong voice assuring me that life continues to blossom well beyond the boundaries of Stage V and midlife transition. I presume that I will probably be faced with another metamorphic rite of passage as the curtain rises on Act III of my life. For now, however, I plan only to think about that possibility and not to write about it.

Labor in Stage V can be long, painful, and complicated. One major obstacle to an easy birth is lack of trust. Some women fear that the Re-Membered Self may emerge from their psychic wombs stillborn, premature, or attached at the heart to a more immature sense of self. They are afraid that their Authentic Adultwoman will fail to thrive in an environment that discounts her wisdom, demeans her gifts, and diminishes her body. Can you imagine Sister Theresa, Toni Morrison, or Beatrice Wood not having faith in themselves and their life's purpose? Another complication is temporary blindness. The birthing-initiate may perceive her infant identity as being fragmented and separate from other living things. To rectify that condition, she must sharpen her inner vision to see beyond such illusions. Through prayer, meditation, and solitude, the midlife mother becomes a mystic. Seen through spiritual eyes, the Re-Membered Self is totally whole and inextricably connected to all things outside of herself. Since the Adultwoman's view of herself is not destined to produce "double vision," her world will not be one of dichotomies and polarities. A third possible complication during the rebirthing process is becoming unconscious. It is essential that the initiate stay awake and alert throughout Stage V. Lack of consciousness could bring about a significant, and perhaps long-lasting, change in her locus of control; someone or something outside of her True Self could take charge of her choices by manipulating her perception of events and people.

A Reflective Exercise

These exercises are intended to help master the task associated with this stage of the Re-Membering rite of passage. They may or may not reinforce some of the strategies described earlier in this chapter. The goal of each one is to encourage you to journey inward and reflect upon the new identity that is taking form. Before you begin, relax your mind and body. Find a comfortable chair or sofa, and then take several deep abdominal breaths. Visualize yourself inhaling serenity and exhaling anxiety. Remember, there is no need to complete these exercises in one sitting or to approach them in sequence. You may want to record your responses in a journal, share them with a friend, or process them with a therapist.

a) Think of what messages our culture associates with the word MATURITY. List any thoughts that pop into your mind. Next, jot down the feelings that are generated by those words. Which of society's attitudes do you think either enhance or impede midlife transition?

b) Assemble a Re-Birthing Bundle in preparation for the birth of your Re-Membered Self. Take walks and collect objects from nature that will assist you during the birthing process. I used a feather, an acorn, a piece of bark, an empty snail shell, a forked twig, and a dried rose bud. I wrapped those "special friends" in a piece of red cloth. My practice was to carry it in my purse and hold it during meditation. In the silence, I was able to hear the faint voices of those esteemed objects. When my time came to deliver, I tried hard to heed their advice.

c) List the times in your life when you have felt either betrayed or abandoned. What circumstances produced those feelings? Have you forgiven the person who betrayed or abandoned you? What good, if any, has come from those events? Has any one trauma been especially helpful to you during this stage of transformation?

d) Write a birth announcement or create a greeting card for your Re-Membered sense of True Self.

e) Draw a portrait of her. In the background, write down words that describe her values, beliefs, interests, image, dreams, and legacy.

f) Identify five mature women, alive or dead, whom you admire. In what ways do they express their authentic identity? What gives them authority? Brainstorm where your Adultwoman will be in five years; ten years. Think about any fears you may have for her well-being.

g) Reflect upon your Merciful Male. Think about his admirable characteristics. Which one do you most admire? Does his presence within you influence your sexuality, goals, feminine nature?

h) Plan a day to celebrate your own Re-Birthday. Do something different or explore a new area of town. Buy yourself a gift that will serve as a memento of this event: for example, a ring, book, piece of pottery. Think of family members, friends, and fairy godmothers you would like to invite to the celebration. Be sure to schedule some time for solitude.

i) Respect your dreams. Write them down and journal about them.

j) Recall your Re-Membering rite of passage. Feel all of the emotions associated with each stage in the process. Draw a picture that symbolizes your midlife dance into middle age.

Ritual for Stage V: Birthing Your Re-Membered Self

This ritual is celebratory in motif. It is intended to help you welcome and embrace your Authentic Adultwoman. In a stylized series of physical and mental actions, you will use energy to make an abstract event more concrete. You will derive the most benefit from the ritual if you prepare your body, mind, and physical setting before you begin. Have the purpose of the ritual clear in your mind. Know that the more you personalize it to fit your history and your taste, the more meaning it will have for you. Feel free to interject your own creativity into this suggested ritual. It is meant to be YOUR celebration. If you decide to conduct it as it appears below, these are the materials that you will need: yellow, white, and blue candles; matches; a long string of yarn; a scissors; the portrait of your Re-Membered Self; a single rose or flower of your choice; an object that will always symbolize this event; and music or poetry of your choice.

Prepare your sacred space by tracing a circle all around it. Next, place the necessary materials on or near the altar. You are now ready to prepare your inner space. Relax your body in a comfortable chair, then quiet your mind by focusing your attention on breathing. Take several deep abdominal breaths. When your inner voice signals readiness, light each candle. As you set flame to the yellow one, think, “My child lights the way.” The white candle carries with it this thought, “My revirginated woman lights the way." With the blue candle, think, "My Merciful Male lights the way." Allow your eyes to devour the flames for a couple of minutes, then close them. Take this seed thought with you into the silence:

SEED THOUGHT:

I am the Mothersoul
I am the Fathermind
I am the Re-Membered One
authentic and whole.

Take the yarn, wrap it around your waist, and tie a knot in it to symbolize the umbilicus. Pick up the self-portrait of your Re-Membered Adultwoman. At this point in the ritual, you may want to name your mature identity. Assume a squatting position. Facing north, let her receive the gifts of gratitude and love. Turn toward the east and allow her to receive wisdom. Face south and gift her with creativity. Finally, look to the north and breathe trust into her.

Still holding the portrait, stand up. Call forth Ariadne's divine presence and protection by saying these invocations aloud:

Invocations

Ariadne, help my Authentic Adultwoman maintain inner balance.

Ariadne, guide her safely into and out of dark places.

Ariadne, prepare her to face death.

Ariadne, restore her trust in the male "other."

Ariadne, teach her the mysteries of transcendence.

Ariadne, strengthen her to stand alone.

Ariadne, connect her to feminine soul.

Ariadne, awaken in her the truth of her divine lineage.

After you place the portrait on the altar, pick up the scissors. Cut the yarn as you affirm this paradox: "In separation I find unity."

Allow all of your senses to "take in" the flower. Consider it a gift to your Re-Membered Self from Mother Nature. Think about its stages of development: seed, bud, blossom. Know that it depends equally on Father Sun and Mother Earth for a balanced diet. Also, its blossom cannot be forced open. Close your eyes and reflect upon ways in which you and the flower are similar.

After a few moments of silence, take your symbolic memento in your hand. Repeat this thought three times, "Through you, I shall remember this day." Finally, welcome your Re-Membered Self with a special song, poem, or dance.

Use a prayer, verse, or special gesture to bring closure to this ritual. Blow out the candles, but save them and burn them on special occasions.

SUMMARY

STAGE V: THE REBIRTH

NATURE GUIDE
A Butterfly

MYTHIC MENTOR
Ariadne

MENTOR QUALITIES
Mediator
Expressive
Knows abandonment
Compassionate
Androgynous
Service-oriented
Ability to empower others
Risk-taking
Experiences mortality/immortality

PRIMARY TASK
To birth your Authentic Adultwoman

PRIMARY STRATEGIES
Become self-observant
Reconnect with nature
Network with peers
Practice solitude
Examine attitudes toward men
Simplify life
Pray and meditate
Celebrate rebirth

MAJOR OBSTACLE(S)
Lack of Trust

RITUAL FOCUS
Celebration

WHOM MIGHT YOU ENCOUNTER?
Your Merciful Male
Your Authentic Adultwoman

POST-INITIATION INVENTORY

You have moved through all five stages of the Re-Membering rite of passage. Read each of the questions below, then place an (X) in the column that reflects your answer.

	Yes	No	?
1. Did you identify losses in your life?	☐	☐	☐
2. Did you reconcile your losses?	☐	☐	☐
3. Did you become a self-observer?	☐	☐	☐
4. Did you identify your "Great Pretenders"?	☐	☐	☐
5. Did you detach from your Superwoman identity?	☐	☐	☐
6. Did you grieve her death?	☐	☐	☐
7. Did you examine your root system?	☐	☐	☐
8. Did you simplify your life?	☐	☐	☐
9. Did you become comfortable with solitude?	☐	☐	☐
10. Did you experience rage?	☐	☐	☐
11. Did you encounter your Eternal Child?	☐	☐	☐
12. Did you encounter your Wise Woman?	☐	☐	☐
13. Did you develop a peer support network?	☐	☐	☐
14. Did you experience death and rebirth?	☐	☐	☐
15. Did your life become more balanced?	☐	☐	☐
16. Did you journey inward?	☐	☐	☐
17. Did you reframe your understanding of midlife?	☐	☐	☐
18. Did you encounter your Supressed Shrew?	☐	☐	☐
19. Did you encounter your Wild Woman?	☐	☐	☐
20. Did you discover your life's purpose?	☐	☐	☐

	Yes	No	?
21. Did you discover your authentic voice?	☐	☐	☐
22. Do you feel connected to other people/things?	☐	☐	☐
23. Do you feel REAL?	☐	☐	☐
24. Did you acquire a sense of service?	☐	☐	☐
25. Did you encounter your Merciful Male?	☐	☐	☐
26. Did you birth your Authentic Adultwoman?	☐	☐	☐
27. Did you discover indwelling feminine gifts?	☐	☐	☐
28. Did you discover your spiritual core?	☐	☐	☐
29. Did you embrace your limitations?	☐	☐	☐
30. Did you heal the mother/daughter wound?	☐	☐	☐
31. Did you come to love yourself?	☐	☐	☐
32. Did you let go of any destructive behavior?	☐	☐	☐
33. Did you become able to laugh at yourself?	☐	☐	☐
34. Do you fear death?	☐	☐	☐
35. Do you look forward to middle age and beyond?	☐	☐	☐
TOTALS	___	___	___

When you finish the inventory, add up the "X"s in each column. Confer with your Wise Woman concerning the outcome. Take special note of your individual "NO" and "?" items. They indicate growth opportunities that await you in the future.

PART III

WHAT IS THE IMPACT OF THE RE-MEMBERING RITE ON RELATIONSHIPS?

In a growing relationship, the original essence is not lost but merely buried under the impedimenta of life. The core of reality is still there and needs only to be increased and reaffirmed.

Anne Morrow Lindbergh
Gifts From the Sea

RELATIONSHIP IS ONE OF the knottiest words in English. Having the chameleon-like quality of changing meaning in response to different contexts, the term mutates with contemporary usage as well as with the past experiences, present circumstances, and future dreams of both sender and receiver. At this very moment, I experience a sense of kinship with animate, inanimate, concrete, and abstract objects. Such relationships run the gamut of connections to God, my daughter, friends, clients, editor, computer, car, and even to my withering Christmas cactus. How can the same word accurately describe the degree of connectedness and depth of interaction that occurs between me and such vastly different kinds of objects? From my point of view, it can't.

Relationships come in many different kinds of wrappings: from a plain brown butcher paper tied with string to a hand-painted watercolor whose uniqueness is further enhanced by satin ribbons. We maintain some relationships to meet the needs of our bodies and minds. Others, we nurture to feed our hearts and souls. As mood rings in pop jewelry respond to body heat, the color of a relationship changes according to its dynamic nature. Relationships take on different hues, forms, and textures over time. They are sensitive not only to minor changes but also to major crises. The purpose of this chapter is to describe the impact that the Re-Membering rite of passage had on both my internal and external worlds of relationships. Each changed dramatically.

As I think about the prickly possibilities in meaning conveyed by the word, "relationship," I recall my days of teaching English as a Second Language to non-English-speaking adults. Many of those beginning students would ask for clarification of a term using this pattern: "Teacher, what means relationship?" Reaching for the answer in *Webster's Seventh*, I would tell them that "relationship" means "the state or character of being related or interrelated." To that gobbledy-gook answer, they would reply, "But, teacher, what means related?" Looking once again to Webster for help, I would explain that "related" can mean different things: "1) connected by relation; 2) allied by kindred; or 3) having a close harmonic connection."[1] Responding to the lost look on most of their faces, I then would return Webster to the shelf, and would define the term using words and examples that were meaningful to my students. For the purpose of this chapter, I want to present a definition of "relationship" that expands upon the abstract nature of Webster's third option and carries personal meaning for me:

> A relationship is an interactive system made up of the flow of energy between two or more objects, and can be maintained through unwritten rules, roles, and routines.

From my perspective, energy is at the core of all relationships. It is that element that brings life, stagnation, death, and dissolution to any personal or professional association. Also, relationships are defined by the "three R's" (rules, roles, and routines). While assumptions concerning those parameters become mutually understood and accepted by the participants over time, changes that a woman experiences during her Re-Membering rite can and usually do create chaos in many of her previously established relationships.

The following are ten statements about relationships and the Re-Membering model of transformation. These "axioms" represent neither psychological nor sociological research findings. Rather, they reflect some simple conclusions drawn from an unstratified random sample of one—me.

AXIOM 1

To relate constitutes a basic human need

A primordial urge exists to unite. This invisible force is evident in all species of plants and animals. If unrecognized or unmet prior to reaching midlife, a human being's need to relate to him/herself as a whole person becomes a prerequisite to sustained growth and to successful aging. While the concepts of individualism, autonomy, and boundaries are celebrated within patriarchal cultures, loneliness, greed and self-aggrandizement assume epidemic proportions. The biased interpretation of separation as a precursor to adulthood is anathema to the individual, familial, communal, and global needs of twenty-first century. Acknowledging our relatedness to, and interdependence upon, all social, political, economic, and environmental systems constitutes humanity's fundamental hope of survival.

AXIOM 2

To relate authentically to others demands that one first relate authentically to oneself

What exactly does the word "authentically" mean? In the context of this book, relating authentically to oneself or others implies the acknowledgement and the acceptance of that which is genuine and true in a person's identity. Women who grow to adulthood in patriarchal societies will evaluate themselves, even their strengths, from a deficit viewpoint.[2] Men, too, have been socialized to accept adulterated assumptions about who they really are. Such misconceptions have a negative impact on relationships.

Authenticity demands that persons identify their own strengths and weaknesses, determine their own values and beliefs, speak in their own voices, act out of their true feelings and claim both the masculine and feminine aspects of their personality.

AXIOM 3

Relationships are complex

Who, what, when, where, why, and how are the ingredients that make relationships difficult to start, to maintain, and to stop. Participants may be casual acquaintances, intimate friends, passionate lovers or business associates, as well as nuclear and extended family members. The list of factors that cause relationships to become knotty includes individual personalities, past experiences, personal values and beliefs, chronological ages, communication styles, stated goals, and unstated expectations.

AXIOM 4

Relationships are vehicles for self-discovery

As I carried out my search for authenticity, I discovered that the journey took me in opposing directions: inward and outward. First, I had to travel on the spiral road that led me back toward my soul's beginning. I journeyed through that terrain in dreams as well as in a wakeful state. During those reflective months, I struggled to exhume, to understand, to surrender, or to integrate several buried aspects of my personality. Those "characters" either had already assumed or were to play major roles in my life's script. A few of my treasured discoveries included "Cookie" the wounded child; "Masterful Male," the perfectionist mentor; "Alma," the Wise Woman; "Rage," my Suppressed Shrew; "Merciful Male," the Dionysian male aspect of my own psyche; and "Faye," the Authentic Adultwoman. In addition to connecting with intrapsychic kinfolk during my inner journey, I also developed supportive relationships with specific goddess guides who helped me maneuver through my Re-Membering rite of passage.

During this same timeframe, I began, sustained, and ended relationships with people and things outside of myself. They, too, gave me the gift of deeper self-insight. I shall describe those relationships in greater detail at a later point in this chapter.

AXIOM 5

Relationships require time, truth, and trust

It seems self-evident that to connect honestly with oneself or with another person requires a conscious commitment of time, honesty, and faith. Initially, I believed that I would zip through my midlife crisis within a few months. Hindsight clearly indicates my sloth-like progress: finding, embracing, and asserting my True Self took me a little more than eight years. As a result of taking a vow of obedience to truth, I was forced to step inside my inner demons, to wrestle with them, and, finally, to accept the revelation that they, too, were part of my "divine ordinariness."[3] Initially, discontentment, disillusionment, and depression were the raw materials of my Re-Membering rite. The childlike faith that I had in an Omnipresent Spirit much greater than myself kept me from running away from my fear or anesthetizing my pain. Instead, the grace of trust made me willing and able to commend my being into invisible but "everlasting arms" during some of the darkest nights of my soul.

AXIOM 6

Relationships largely define a woman's sense of identity

"Spider is the female energy of the creative force that weaves the beautiful designs of life."[4] The arachnid symbolizes a woman's ability to spin an intricate web of affiliations. Relationships at the center of her web as well those along its edges provide reflections from which she creates her own sense of identity. The problem that I encountered as "Spiderwoman" was double edged: I understood neither who I really was, nor how I was to relate to those who shared my web. As a result, I became entangled in a web of illusion that distorted my ability to respect myself and to honor those around me. For a large portion of time during the Re-Membering rite, I was compelled to ignore or to withdraw from many of the relationships that I had woven. Actually, I needed to turn most of my attention upon myself and to devour parts of whom I had been. Not until I ate my Synthetic Superwoman image was I able to grasp momentary glimpses of my True Self.

AXIOM 7

Women have been socialized to "Not Make Waves" and to "Be the Glue" in relationships

As a child, I had learned this lesson well: good girls are nice girls, nice girls are acquiescent girls, acquiescent girls are loveable. As I blossomed, so did that injunction. Finally, I came to this understanding about its meaning: loveable girls are responsible, responsible girls "don't rock the boat"—they "hang in there" even during stormy weather.

My seventh edition of Webster's dictionary presents these synonyms for "responsible": answerable; accountable; amenable; and liable. All of those lexical items imply that a responsible person is subjected either to review or to control by a designated authority figure. In my life, that person has worn many different faces: a parent, a child, a spouse, a friend, a lover, an employer, or an employee. There have been times, too, when I have felt accountable to faceless objects, including my career goals, my mortgage payments, and my eternal soul. Examining Webster's definition further, I discovered that one of the synonyms for "responsibility" was "burden."[5] With hindsight, I see clearly how my sense of responsibility became not only burdensome, but it also became self-abusive. I had accepted the status quo in an emotionally destructive relationship and had stayed in it far too long. Repeatedly, either to maintain my sanity or perhaps to survive, I restrained my urges to stir up its toxic waters. Within our gender-biased society, women must be on guard not to impede their individual growth and risk their personal safety with misconceived notions about stormy seas and responsible anchors.

Specifically at midlife, I experienced tidal-sized waves of change. Instead of riding their crests into a halcyon bay where I could spawn myself into middle age, I instinctively chose, like the salmon, to follow a treacherous, solitary, upstream path. During that journey, my body, mind, heart, and soul became battered on psychological boulders, and my over-developed sense of responsibility became unglued in the swift-moving currents. The lessons shared with me by the salmon were about the fluid nature of life's cycles, the fetal waters of birth, the cleansing energy of initiation, the upstream battle for gender equity, and the death and rebirth mysteries that embody the Re-Membering rite of passage. Especially at that transformational time in her life, a woman needs to risk making waves and to let herself become unglued.

AXIOM 8

Initiates in the Re-Membering rite relate horizontally and vertically to each stage of the model

After a few false starts and painful detours within each stage of the process, I realized that I had to move not only horizontally but also vertically when excavating my "Re-Membering dig." I learned quickly to identify and to appreciate the artifacts that lay close to the surface of my conscious awareness. The real treasures, however, were buried deep within the stratified layers of repressed memories and times past. I felt more confident and less vulnerable when I was exploring the parts of my identity that had been more exposed to external elements. Those within the darkest recesses of my psychic tomb took the longest to exhume and were the most painful and the scariest to examine. Because I had to move in two directions through each stage of the model, time soon became an irrelevant factor when it came to assessing my overall progress.

AXIOM 9

Relationship with the True Self is the goal of the Re-Membering Rite

Carl Gustav Jung saw the development of the conscious personality, the ego, evolving during childhood and youth. He saw the unconscious personality, the True Self, demanding attention around midlife and evolving throughout the second half of life. According to Jung, "the Self is the center and psychic life revolves around it .... The Self becomes the source of energy, the motivating force, the energizer, the healer, the reason for being, the integrating force bringing the conscious and the unconscious into wholeness."[6] The True Self's initial call may take the form of an intermittent whisper; however, time changes both the volume and the frequency. The True Self is latent in the unconscious mind of today's Synthetic Superwoman (and Synthetic Superman). It is implicit there and represents the embodiment of her divine potentialities and human possibilities. An initiate in the Re-Membering rite becomes sensitive to a missing element within her sense of identity or conscious personality. By focusing her attention inward and surrendering to the gravitational pull of the downward spiral, each participant reorients herself spiritually. Eventually, she reconnects with and embraces her divine nature, whose feminine and masculine aspects are perfectly balanced.

AXIOM 10

Relationships become strained during the Re-Membering Rite of Passage

Human beings struggle with relationships during midlife because they either need to recast their comfy-cozy mask of identity or to stagnate throughout the second half of life. As the Synthetic Superwoman reweaves her relational web into one of "self-is-ness," she is sure to hurt some of the people who had shared the former web with her, to anger others, to make a few grow stronger, to cause some to abandon her, and to let a very small number fall through the gaping holes. Threads of the "self-is-ness" web create an unique configuration because the initiate spins them from her authentic values, core beliefs, personal interests, and Re-Membered identity.

> *Our whole life is a movement toward ourself, others, and God.*
>
> Janice Brewi and Anne Brennan
> *Mid-Life: Psychological and Spiritual Perspectives*

THE RE-MEMBERING PROCESS AND MY RELATIONSHIP TO MYSELF

This morning, Lake Como was dressed for the first time in her "winter whites." While my boots crunched along the snow-packed path, my conversation with Mother Nature was interrupted repeatedly by the cawing of a substantial crow. Neither Mother Nature nor I deferred to the bird's insistent noise. I was stopped short, however, when Crow left her observation tower atop a naked tree, landed on the sidewalk just in front of me, and began to dance with her shadow. This winged messenger had a secret she wanted to share with me. When I returned home, I read this about Crow medicine:

> ... Crow can bend the laws of the physical universe and "shape shift." This art includes doubling, or being in two places at one time consciously; taking on another physical form, and becoming the "fly on the wall" to observe what is happening far away ... Crow is an omen of change ... Crow merges light and darkness, seeing both inner and outer reality ... You must put aside your fear of being a voice in the wilderness and "caw" the shots as you see them ... Shape shift that old reality and become your future self.[8]

As that description of Crow simmered in my mind, I began to draw parallels between what I had just read in *Medicine Cards* and what I had experienced during the Re-Membering process. Like Crow, I danced with my shadow, merged light and darkness within myself, saw inner and outer reality, punctured illusions, became a fly on the walls of my own mind, and shape shifted old realities of myself through a variety of psychological transformations.

In the next few pages, I will describe how my relationship with myself changed as I sorted out the tangled skein of midlife Re-Membering. To do that, I will first look at the specific dimensions of identity, behaviors, and feelings within each of the five stages of the Re-Membering process. Next, I will explore changes that took place in my perceptions of these concepts: male/female principle; time; space; change; choice; sexuality; spirituality; life; middle age; and death.

Re-Membering and My Identity

Stage I: The Wounds

Were I to choose a symbol to describe my identity at the initial stage of Re-Membering myself, it would be a question mark. Up to that time, I had felt comfortable with the identity of Synthetic

Superwoman because that illusion had served me well. Not until I began to travel mentally to times past and to cross the borders back into my childhood did I begin to experience the first twinges of dismemberment. On one of my first "nature talks" around Lake Como, I came upon a rock that resembled half a grapefruit. That shape intrigued me because, on the flat surface, there was a deep depression that looked as if a large segment had been eaten. Now, that rock sits on my prayer table because it was largely responsible for starting me on my journey. It forced me to ask these key questions: "What part of me is missing?" and "Where do I go to find it?" Over the next several months I focused on reconnecting with "Cookie," the playful and innocent childlike part of myself that was abandoned four decades earlier. In the hard and humbling task of trying to reconcile with that child, my Superwoman image began to feel too tight, too unbalanced, too false, too disconnected, and too ego-driven. Within a couple of weeks, it began to shrivel.

Changes in my behavior provided me (and others) with ample evidence that something strange had begun to happen inside of me. My sleep became interrupted more frequently by disturbing dreams. I lost my desire to eat wisely and filled up the gastric void with fast foods. I began to disassemble the routines and the rules that I had established in parenting, working, homemaking, and socializing. Unfocused "busyness" and unmeaningful tasks began to fill my daily To Do List. Although I lacked the understanding and the words to describe what was happening to me, actions and feelings convinced me of its significance.

The longer and the more honestly I communicated with Cookie, my eternal child, I discovered that feelings about who I was were in a state of flux. My self-confidence seemed to be unraveling. Sadness and resentment dogged me day and night. My body felt tired, my mind felt confused, and my heart felt unentitled to even the simplest expressions of pleasure and happiness. In spite of my hard-won successes, I felt like a loser.

Only after I had mastered the task of Stage I, to identify past losses and wounds that disconnected me from my feminine core, was I able to move forward into the next stage of the Re-Membering rite.

Stage II: The Dying

My identity as Synthetic Superwoman moved through the process of dying in Stage II. It was then that the "I" of my hard-won identity became animated much as a computer graphic. It moved in two opposing directions and turned into my symbol for Stage II, the letter "X". That letter marked the spot in time when I died unto my former sense of self. By deciding "to pull the plug" on Synthetic Superwoman, I unmasked key elements within that assumed identity. Consciously, I declined to give "Helpless Victim," "Masterful Male" and "Perfect Mom" further sustenance. The inauthentic, competitive, and outer-oriented nature of my synthetic sense of self intensified during that time.

In Stage II, my "Observer Self" witnessed a continuous breakdown of routines, rules, and roles. Interrupted sleep patterns graduated into full-blown anxiety attacks. The ingestion of fast food was followed by stomach upset and pain. By moving into an even faster lane, I thought I might anesthetize the pain in my life.

The negative feelings that I experienced in Stage II became more aggravated during The Dying stage. Hurt turned into depression, resentment became anger, fatigue became exhaustion, vulnerability became a defect, and self-pity became self-criticism.

In my journal entries, the words "dying" and "fear" appeared on a regular basis. The notion of living life without my Superwoman façade left me feeling afraid that I would dissolve into dust. With the dying of my ego-driven allies, I gained first-hand understanding of this reality: theoretical identities were, are, and always will be dust.

Stage III: The Death

My identity during this stage could be summed up in the numerical symbol "0." I thought of myself as having become a person with no identity, a nonentity. My ego-driven compulsion to achieve came to a halt with a definitive thud. Burnout and depression stalked me around the clock. When I hit the wall of reality, the remains of Synthetic Superwoman had vaporized and had floated away in the air. My identity became transitory; I was a phantom of my former self.

During Stage III, all of my activities felt forced. Sleep became my preferred mode of escape. The action verb "to do" was adversarial to my compelling need "to be." I stopped following familiar rules and routines. Fun and socializing were only intermittent blips on my life's monitor. I could no longer be seduced back into animation by food, fun, or friends. In the footsteps of fictitious Alice, I had tumbled down my own dark spiral tunnel.

My Observer Self stood at attention as Superwoman lay in state. I consciously grieved her death because I had worked so long and so hard to breathe life into her. Besides, she had become my good friend. Especially during Stage III, I resonated to Ann Keiffer's self-description of feeling "like a blown-out egg."[9] All of my nerve endings felt raw and exposed. I saw my depression turn into despair, my anger intensify into rage, my loneliness develop into isolation, and my self-criticism become self-contempt.

The task to be mastered in this stage was to detach from my former sense of self. In the sanctuary of solitude, I encountered two soulmates: Alma, my Wise Woman, and Rage, my Suppressed Shrew. For months, a psychic war ensued between those two aspects of my personality. Before moving into Stage IV, I had to allow each one sufficient opportunity to take charge and to assume center stage in my midlife melodrama.

Stage IV: The Gestation

Like a mother duck sitting on a full nest, I understood my role during Stage IV of the transformation process. An arrow from Artemis' quiver symbolizes how I saw myself during this hatching time. I realized that I had been disassembled and that my individual parts would soon be placed on an invisible assembly line. My purposeful inward orientation created the outward perception of selfishness. I identified with the idea of being pregnant with myself.

Throughout Stage IV, I was determined to practice good prenatal care. I engaged in activities that nurtured my body, mind, and spirit, as well as the new life that was taking form within my psychic womb. Weeks were spent daydreaming and defining beliefs, values, interests, and goals that reflected the Re-Membering me. I scheduled activities in a way that integrated and maintained a sense of balance and structure in my life. Gradually, I began to socialize, but chose primarily to be in the company of women. I made a conscious commitment to eat nutritiously "for two." Sleep became the vehicle that transported me to the world of my dreams. While in that creative void, I continued to commune with what I came to call my "SHEtus," the fetal mass of my Authentic Adultwoman.

Although I was still psychologically cocooned, the anticipation of a Re-Membered birthday made me feel hopeful and happy. I began to feel more vibrant physically and emotionally. Having expended a great deal of energy in depression and rage, I was able now to regenerate my vitality through the feminine gifts of creativity and imagination. I felt the connection to my True Self grow steadily stronger.

Stage V: The Re-Birth

Although I can recall wanting to pant and to push my new identity into existence, her journey through the birth canal was long and labored. At last, on an unspecified day and at an unspecified hour, a joyful voice within me whispered, "she's here."

Because the circle represents wholeness, I claim it to symbolize my identity in Stage V. This was the profile of my "midlife miracle" that I described in my journal: "She is a Self-driven, balanced, interdependent, cooperative, self-loving, Re-Membered human being. The expression in her eyes simultaneously reflects the three fates—past, present, and future. With that wisdom, she admits to having found Shekhinah, a Hebrew word meaning the feminine face of God."

My infant identity slept soundly and ate heartily. Like a toddler, she reached out to life with trust and curiosity. Her energy seemed limitless; in fact, I began to think of her as being a spirited child or an "active alert."[10] Wanting to live in the state of grace, the behavior of my Authentic Adultwoman revolved around these gifts of the Spirit: simplicity, solitude, and spontaneity.

As a result of the Re-Membering rite of passage, my mature identity became one that felt entitled to inner peace, pleasure, and prosperity. In her renewed virginal state, she took the vows of authenticity, gratitude, and service. She continues to feel secure in knowing that her power and glory reside within herself; that is, her True Self is soul-bound where it always was, is now, and will be forever.

Re-Membering and My Point of View

In an epigraph, Jean Lanier shares this thought: "In the beginning everything was in relationship, and in the end everything will be in relationship again. In the meantime, we live by hope."[11] In 1990, as I began Re-Membering myself, I viewed life much as would a person with astigmatism. Through cultural conditioning, my perception of several basic concepts had become blurred and unfocused. Because of that learned defect, my relationship to the idea of a male/female principle, time, space, choice, change, sexuality, spirituality, life, and death had become unbalanced. As hope accompanied me through the rite of passage, I discovered that both my distorted understanding and blurred vision of those ideas gradually became corrected. I will use the next few paragraphs to describe what that correction entailed.

Male/female principle

The male-female dichotomy lies at the base of the Re-Membering process. Imprisoning both men and women, this malevolent jailer inflicts deep and perhaps irrevocable wounds on the process of identity formation in members of both genders. Institutions within our western culture laud and reflect the androcentric or male principle. Like many Synthetic Superwomen, somewhere along my journey to adulthood I picked up the notion and the need to become a "pseudo-male." I grew to revere alpha qualities such as these: analytical, independent, mind-centered, active, dominating, strong, and competitive. Intending to become a "success," I turned my back on these feminine or beta traits described as intuitive, dependent, heart-centered, passive, weak, and cooperative. My successful passage into middle age and beyond demanded that I heal the psychological gash that split my original sense of wholeness in two.

Over the course of the Re-Membering rite, my relationship to these two concepts changed radically. In the initial stages, I discovered that instead of holding the male principle in high esteem, I resented, feared, and even hated that aspect within my own personality. As I rediscovered and embraced my repressed feminine nature, the male aspect within my own psyche changed from that of an abusive, demeaning, and demanding patriarch into a refined and redefined "inner man of the heart."[12] As a Re-Membered Adultwoman, I no longer relate to these principles with a binary sense of vision. Instead, I view them as being bi-polar but interdependent aspects on the continuum labeled gender.

Time

Because of a distorted image of time, I had lived most of my young adult life in the ambiance of a pressure cooker. The beat of my "Synthetic Superwoman's" heart became synchronized to the inviolable ticks of the clock. I got up long before Grandfather Sun stretched his arms over the horizon, and I went to bed long after Grandmother Moon wrapped her indigo blanket around this half of planet Earth. I used time either to turn a To Do List into a litany of lies or to cultivate stress-producing complexities. I related to time as if it were a finite element that belonged to someone other than to me. Time for myself always felt "borrowed" and seemed to be laced with guilt. My blurred vision of time fostered fragmentation in my life instead of unification. It forced me to focus on "doing" rather than on "being."

After falling through the chronological crack of midlife crisis, my relationship to time changed—the pressure cooker turned into a crockpot. With a more hope-filled relationship to time, I began to simplify my life in order to sustain my sanity. I streamlined the To Do List and designated time for myself as a high-priority item. I cut out a lot of complexity by making frequent use of the one-syllable word, "no." I shed my Seiko for a designated period of time, and I began to move to the tempo and the rhythm of Mother Nature's cyclical symphony. When depending more on nature to choreograph the steps of my life's dance, I reassessed our culture's three-dimensional perspective on time. Having reconciled much of the "unfinished business" in my past, I decided to focus on the present and to live in the momentary sense of NOW. Present time became a seedbed in which I sowed futuristic ideas, goals, and dreams. As such, time was no longer an external element that wielded power over me. On the contrary, by relating to time from an internal point of view, I not only gained control over it but also melted into it.

Space

My dictionary presents fewer than ten definitions of the word "space."[13] Some of them emphasize these attributes: distance, dimension, and degree. The most significant way in which my relationship to the concept of space changed, following the Re-Membering rite of passage, was that space took on an aura of sacredness.

As I stood at midlife's threshold, my ideas about what space was and how it ought to be used were muddled. On one hand, I thought of space as a "boundaryless" three-dimensional expanse. For a joke, on my forty-fifth birthday, colleagues gave me a 12" X 12" square of floor tile. The poignant message they meant to convey was that, at long last, Kathleen would have a physical area to call her own either at home or at work. I had no practical grasp of the relationship between space and boundaries. On the other hand, space was a lexical reference to areas outside of my own physical body. In the past, my own naivete had allowed others to invade or to penetrate my sacred space. On still another level, I ascribed this meaning to the term "space": either a concrete or an abstract void that was to be filled up with something. I felt compelled to saturate my schedule with business appointments, personal errands, and social events. I seemed unable to relax, and felt particularly uncomfortable being just with myself. While beckoning to me, solitude was frightening.

As I followed the Re-Membering rite's spiral path, I acquired a different point of view concerning space. All dimensions of my personal being, even the shadows, became sacred. As such, they demanded respect from me and from others. In addition to space outside myself, I began to acknowledge my internal space; that part of me in which resided my mind, dreams, intuition, creativity, and soul. Extensions outside myself became sacred as well: my home, my workspace, my family members, friends, and community. No space was to be desecrated by counter-productive thoughts, words, or actions. With a broadened perception of space, I developed a sense of clarity concerning the concept of boundaries. I continue to work hard building and maintaining them in physical settings as well as in personal relationships. Paradoxically, my ability to establish boundaries was enhanced only after I realized the degree to which no boundaries separated me from other people and from other things. Finally, empty space or solitude no longer scares me. I have come to recognize it as being a primary nutrient for my continued growth. Now, my body, mind, heart, and spirit crave the serene space that I know as solitude.

Choice

If I were to symbolize the idea of choice, I would select the diamond-shaped decision point found in a flowchart. When, as Superwoman, I was confronted with a major or a minor decision, the centrifugal force generated by my sense of responsibility to others consistently pulled me away from choices that reflected my needs, wishes, or points of view. Hindsight indicates how my perspective about choice caused me to feel invisible. Systematically, Superwoman performed radical surgery on her choice options because of her perfectionism, need for approval, and fear of both failure and success.

A prerequisite for completing the Re-Membering rite of passage was that I identify beliefs, values, goals, and interests that reflected the "Real Me." Armed with that information, I made a concerted effort to utilize it when faced with making choices throughout the transition process. As I surrendered my need to be perfect and to be liked, the brilliant sparkle of my "humble humanness" illumined the choices I made. As a result, I approached life's decision points with love and not with fear.

Change

During the late sixties, I believed these lyrics as I sang them: "To everything turn, turn, turn. There is a season, turn, turn, turn. And a time for every purpose under heaven." I thought that I understood and accepted the inevitability of change in the life cycle. However, when midlife crisis pounded on my door, I tried hard to deny, diminish, and delay the myriad changes that accompanied it. While my Superwoman identity often made me feel as if I were wearing an undersized pair of pantyhose, I was resistant to admitting that I had outgrown the old "knickers." Moreover, I was reluctant to even try on a different size or style. At midlife, I became disoriented by the volume of change that seemed to be avalanching around me and I was afraid of its intensity.

An outcome of the Re-Membering process is successful maturation. That goal requires an initiate to negotiate the idea of change from a new point of view. Changes at midlife bring to the fore the critical choice between creative growth or self-limiting stagnation. As I reassembled myself and prepared for a rebirth, my perspective on change evolved into one that viewed change in these ways: 1) a vehicle for clearing away clutter; 2) a strategy toward self-understanding; 3) a catalyst for continued learning; and 4) a tool to design a hope-filled future.

Sexuality

I must confess that prior to completing the Re-Membering rite of passage, this Virgo writer would have felt reluctant to address any "X-rated" issue—especially sex—in written form. As a precocious member of a strict Roman Catholic family, I had drawn three important conclusions about sex before I had made my First Holy Communion: 1) having sex could sometimes make a baby; 2) it was always a scary, naughty "no-no"; and 3) touching or looking at my "privates" could make me a sick, dirty, and sinful kid. Even before I had outgrown the magical kingdom of childhood, I had begun unconsciously to reject and even to revile the most obvious expressions of my female gender. As a budding adolescent, I became a more conscious co-conspirator in society's undeclared war against females' sexuality. My menstrual cycle became "the curse," feminine hygiene and fat became obsessions, breasts became natural adversaries to brains, and sex became synonymous to intercourse, which, of course, became sacred and safe only after marriage.

In spite of the years she blossomed in graduate school, my Superwoman's understanding of her own sexuality withered because it was rooted in fear, shame, and guilt. For decades she was a borderline "emotional anorexic"; that is, she starved herself of touch and of tenderness. Life's simple pleasures of physical bonding and sexual intimacy were minimized while she pursued professional recognition and achievement. With her vulnerability intensified by young widowhood as well as by an emotionally abusive relationship, celibacy became an easy lifestyle for my Synthetic Superwoman to choose.

Through almost all of the Re-Membering rite of passage, I chose to be celibate. I lacked the trust, the time, the energy, the interest, as well as the need to be sexual in a relationship. Instead, I focused on reassembling myself and on keeping my revirginating psyche physically and emotionally intact. Self-reflection indicates that my relationship to sex and to sexuality changed only after my sense of identity became androgynous or gender-balanced. Finally, having accepted and loved both the masculine and the feminine parts of myself, I took back my body. I began to appreciate my cyclical connection to the moon, my biochemical relationship to the stars, and my empowering legacy from ancient goddesses. At that point, I became able and willing to surrender to a sexual relationship with another person. Ultimately, intimacy and spirituality became the joyful twins produced from the union of my whole authentic self with that other individual.

Spirituality

From the time I was very young, I expressed more than casual curiosity about the life of the spirit. For over two decades, organized religion provided the structure through which I exercised my search for the divine. As a youngster, I had accumulated an enviable collection of Holy Cards, and I spent hours devouring biographies of mystics and martyrs. In late adolescence, I heard a quiet calling from within to walk a contemplative's path in this life. My challenge, however, was to follow that mandate outside monastic walls. Within the secular halls of academia, I divested myself of Catholicism, and I began to explore ideas of a divine essence beyond those described in Christianity. It was not until midlife, however, that I commenced my commitment to spirituality as a way of life.

As I tip-toed into my Re-Membering rite of passage, I felt compelled to explore this question: What is spirituality? Janice Brewi and Anne Brennan provided this answer in their book, *Celebrate Mid-life*[14]: "One's spirituality is the way one lives one's life .... It is the spilling out of an inner reality. It is the incarnation of the spirit."

As I reconciled historical wounds, confronted inner demons, reframed traumas, heeded nature's wisdom, and surrendered my Superwoman identity, I experienced a revolutionary reorientation of focus. That shift in gravity—away from an ego-based understanding of religion toward a soul-based recognition of the divine potential within my inner core—resulted in spiritual maturation. In my fourth decade of life, I stopped seeing myself as a saintly child of God. Instead, I started living as a wholly human adult woman whose sacred feminine spirit would unfold through a conscious communion with a Divine Being. Following that imperative, I have taken the vows of obedience, chastity, and balance; that is, I honor my inner voice, keep my True Self intact, and maintain a sense of equity between my male and female nature. My midlife view of spirituality has allowed me to enjoy these delicious fruits of the Spirit: forgiveness, trust, gratitude, good humor, hope, wisdom, spontaneity, simplicity, solitude, imagination, humility, unity, and self-acceptance.

Midlife

Over a century ago, Carl Jung observed that most forty-year-olds were wholly unprepared to embark on the second half of life. Moreover, colleges were unable to prepare them adequately to meet the demands of life's afternoon segment.[15] Contemporary forty-year-olds are faced with much the same dilemma. The situation today may be even more dramatic because of our extended lifespan and our emphasis on youth. The trauma associated with midlife becomes intensified as a result of cultural misinterpretations and educational oversight. As child, adolescent, and young adult, I gobbled up and digested many of society's misconceptions about midlife. Some of the most widely accepted inaccuracies are embedded in birthday card greetings for "the poor unfortunate souls" turning 40-plus. These ideas may have a ring of familiarity:

> You're over the hill and ready for the compost pile.
>
> Love and libido are "intermittent blips" on your life's monitor.
>
> The "grim reaper" is gaining on you.
>
> The empty nest is a lonely nest.
>
> Gravity resculpts your body.
>
> Dementia assaults your brain.
>
> Dreams grow moldy and die.
>
> Midlife means crises.

At midlife, people stand before a closed door that ushers them into the second half of their lives. For some time, I envisioned that door as resembling one on the exterior of a mausoleum: it opened up onto a dark and musty-smelling interior where life stopped and death reigned. Over the course of Re-Membering myself, I assumed a more positive perspective about this liminal time of life: an empty wasteland became fertile farmland in which I cultivated my authentic identity. My midlife adventure took me inward on a "holy pilgrimage."[16] During that time of questing and of questioning, I rewrote the past and the future of my life's story by reclaiming my feminine soul in the present. As a result, midlife became a gateway into the realization of my full potential. It was a time when I became an unconscious alchemist and turned the lead of depression into the gold of wholeness. In midlife, I became intimate with my True Self, entitled to my sense of integrity, and committed to my image as a generative Adultwoman.

Life and Death

Because I have always embraced the concept of an afterlife, the word "life" carries two major meanings in my personalized dictionary: 1) life represents the duration of an earthly existence; and 2) it describes the spiritual existence that transcends physical death.

For years, I have equated a person's experience of living life to that of a student moving through an individualized curriculum. The educational institution in which I see all animate (and inanimate) objects to be registered is planet earth. As our bodies and souls evolve, life presents us with events that determine whether or not we master specific cognitive, affective, and spiritual competencies. Sometimes we "breeze through" a test. In fact, we might even have fun taking it. Examples of some of those types of testing situations include taking a trip, having a child, getting married, being promoted, buying a new car or home, starting college, completing a goal, or winning the lottery. At other times, we might totally "blow it." Frequently, mastery tests are disguised as traumatic circumstances: chronic or terminal illness, addictions, economic failure, infertility, divorce, war, poverty, geographic moves, retirement, death, and midlife crisis. Because lessons within the curriculum of each individual's life are personalized, the frequency and the difficulty level of each mastery test becomes unique.

During the first half of my life, I considered life and death to be opposites of one another. Following my Re-Membering rite, I have come to see aspects of each event reflected in the other. Below are a few characteristics shared by both life and death:

They move the participant into an unknown realm.

They are creative events.

They demand surrender.

They are events of self-discovery.

They are intimate events.

They are growth-producing.

They can be initiations.

They may occur in a hospital, at home, or anywhere.

They may generate feelings of loss.

They may be painful.

I visualize an incarnating soul, prior to the birth experience, spending its gestation time "getting dressed" for the occasion; that is, properly arranging its organs, bones, temperament, and skin. In the process of dying, that same incarnated soul will "disrobe" or drop its earth-bound body and personality. When pregnant with my daughter, I felt life for the first time while flying to Alaska at an altitude of 40,000 feet. Experiencing her development within me, as well as her birth, were mastery tests presented to me by the transpersonal professor, Dr. Life. As Synthetic Superwoman, I passed both of those exams with "flying colors" and celebrated my success in public. Four months later, as I removed the wedding ring from my husband's hand and gave hospital staff permission to stop all life support efforts, Superwoman realized that Dr. Life was with her at Barry's bedside. Unlike the mastery test associated with life and birth, the competencies related to death and bereavement took Superwoman almost a decade to pass. In fact, she died, in private, grieving her failed attempts. As I reflect upon my views about life and death, I realize that the traumatic tests of childbirth and of spousal death were the two key events that pushed me through the defined edges of my manufactured sense of self. Mastery of the tasks associated with life and death gave Synthetic Superwoman permission to die. Eventually, that void was transformed into the womb in which I Re-Membered my Authentic Adultwoman.

THE RE-MEMBERING PROCESS AND MY RELATIONSHIP TO OTHERS

Think for a moment of what happens to the surface of a calm lake when a stone, even a very small one, shatters its mirror-like appearance. After swallowing the tiny morsel, the water begins to hiccup spasmodically in concentric circles. In much the same way, the changes that a woman experiences during her Re-Membering rite of passage extend outward from her like invisible fingers. They leave their indelible prints on all the relationships that exist within her affiliative web. The purpose of this part of the chapter is to describe how my relationship to other people and to important things in my life were affected by the Re-Membering rite.

My Daughter

In spite of the twenty-three hours of hard labor that I endured awaiting her arrival, my daughter's birthday is one of the few days of my life that I would care to relive. Representing my husband's gift of love to me, she is an energetic body of evidence that supports my belief in the transcendence of life over death.

Before the reassembling of myself at midlife, my Superwoman identity required that I also be Supermom. In trying to play that role convincingly, I sabotaged myself and short-changed my child. While chopping a path through the uncharted territory of single motherhood, I intuitively did many things well. However, honesty demands that I admit to making many "thumbs-down decisions," especially concerning the art of "adult" parenting. Superwoman demanded perfection, suppressed feelings, feigned strength, practiced inconsistency, and communicated unclearly. With hindsight's 20/20 vision, I see myself acting and hear myself speaking inauthentically during a great deal of my daughter's first decade. Because my identity as an Authentic Adultwoman had not yet emerged, I felt uncertain of how to approach the role of "mom" from that perspective.

As I moved through the Re-Membering rite, my mother-daughter relationship became especially strained. Wrestling with depression's darkest demons, I felt myself less and less able to cope with her hypersensitive and hyperintense temperament. I feared that if despair did not devour me, the demands associated with around-the-clock single-parenting a high-spirited child would bring about that same unhappy ending.

Finally, when I surrendered my Superwoman image to the realm of fantasy, my body and my mind began to secrete a healing balm that I applied to a relationship that had become chronically irritated. Given education, time, and effort, I learned to maintain appropriate boundaries with my daughter, to speak to her clearly and consistently in one voice, to establish realistic expectations for both of us, and to laugh at my maternal shortcomings. As a Re-Membered woman, I have grown into a Re-Membered mom. Now, I am able to assume that role with authority, confidence, serenity, and humor.

My Mother

In *The Heroine's Journey*, Maureen Murdock devotes an entire chapter to what she calls " the mother/daughter split."[17] Like most of my high-achieving sisters, I separated from the feminine or "motherly-type" aspects of my psyche as a very young child. However, my emancipation from my personal mother was not complete until I moved through the Re-Membering rite of passage.

Being the middle child, I slid most naturally into the family position of "responsible golden girl." Doctors at the Mayo Clinic diagnosed my father's illness as acute rheumatoid arthritis. That diagnosis coincided with my brother's birth. Seemingly overnight, one anticipated but three uninvited boarders moved in with us. No one ever spoke openly about the latter three, but we all adapted to the invisible presence of Fear, Anger, and Pain. When my mother took a full-time job outside the home, my individual exodus from childhood was hastened.

In those years, I spent no time grieving that loss. I wanted to ease my parents' burdens. We all worked especially hard to minimize the demands that were placed on my father and to see that his needs were met. My mother came to symbolize a protective fortress in which I sought stability and security. My admiration for her strength, tenacity, drive, logic, objectivity, and follow-through increased with each birthday that I celebrated. In time, I became a "parentified child," intent on helping my over-worked mother and pleasing my sick father.

When, as a child, I explored the question, "What does it mean to be a woman?" I guessed at possible answers. I watched my mother function in that role as an asexual, over-responsible, other-oriented, bionic human being. Given her personal history as well as the circumstances in our home, my mother had lost herself in the affiliative web she wove around "others." Needing to keep her feminine gifts "in check," she fine-tuned her masculine skills. Sitting at her right hand, I tried to emulate many of those qualities in order to keep the family happy and "the home fires burning." On one hand, my mother's masculine-oriented characteristics were instrumental in helping me attain my academic and my professional goals. On the other hand, they reinforced this destructive pattern: ignoring the feminine side of my nature. Thus, I split away from that part of myself, became unbalanced, and generated the "pseudo-male" identity of Synthetic Superwoman. How paradoxical that by pleasing my biological father and by admiring my biological mother, the authentic "I" in my identity became invisible.

Stumbling down the spiral path of Re-Membering, I rediscovered aspects of that "I." To reclaim them, I had to become fully separated from my personal mother. It was necessary for me to sort out from hers the values, interests, and beliefs that reflected me. As I tried to find and to speak in my own voice, our relationship experienced more frequent periods of discord. Like a sleeping volcano, feelings of suppressed anger toward her (and my father) began to rumble deep inside me. Finally, with the help of a therapist, they erupted. I screamed out red-hot rage from the deepest part of me. Beneath those ashes, however, I healed the psychological mother/daughter split, severed the invisible umbilicus between me and my personal mother, and sowed more seeds of my Authentic Adultwoman. Still admiring her masculine-graced qualities, it pleases me to see my mother nurturing the feminine side of herself much more in retirement. Now, as a Re-Membered woman, I love and honor her as the love-wise and creative crone that she is.

Other Women

For almost three decades, I have called myself a feminist. Because that label engenders a variety of images, I want to clarify my use of it before I describe the impact of midlife Re-Membering on my relationships with other women. From my point of view, feminism is a way of perceiving one's own reality as well as that of the whole world. My understanding of the concept concurs with the definition that Kathleen Fischer presents in her book, *Women at the Well:* "Feminism is a vision of life emphasizing inclusion rather than exclusion, connectedness rather than separateness, the mutuality in relationships rather than dominance and submission. Feminism also entails the conviction that full individual development can take place only within a human community that is structured in justice."[18]

During what I considered to be unjust times—the turbulent sixties—I personalized my understanding of feminism and I branded myself a feminist. At that same time, however, I began acting like a misguided sculptor—molding my "honorary man" mentality into the figure of Superwoman and casting the "manufactured mask" that someday would conceal my fatigue, fear, anger, and depression. I made a clear break from the supportive bonds of sisterhood while in graduate school. Over several years in that environment, I had searched for a feminist mentor, only to discover that my potential candidates had been stricken with "Queen Bee Syndrome." Instead of helping me move forward, they systematically sabotaged my progress. In spite of labeling myself a feminist, my relationship to other women became tainted by that experience and by male-oriented misperceptions concerning the feminine psyche. In time, I learned to compete aggressively with other women, to mistrust their competencies, to envy their gifts, to fear their victories, and to disassociate myself from those who were involved in careers that lacked professional status. As a "Super Spiderwoman," I felt compelled to nurture those relationships within my web that would bring me recognition, power, status, and financial independence.

The midlife experiences of bringing forth life from my womb and of removing my mythic mask presented me with two precious gifts: a perfectly-formed baby daughter and a Re-Membered perspective on feminism. My conscience was piqued by the deceit that I felt in embracing a feminist philosophy while ignoring my own feminine gifts and mistrusting those in other women. As I began to acknowledge and to celebrate the talents within myself, my relationship to other women began to change. For example, I came to realize that, as "loving listeners," women can help initiate each other into various life stages and circumstances: middle age, widowhood, single parenthood, empty nests, elder care, and old age. We hear unspoken cries for help, bleed beyond our personal boundaries, permit our bodies to be penetrated for the sake of the future, implant the seeds of tomorrow within the walls of our wombs, guide the incarnating soul as well as the dying body into new realms of reality, and weave into humanity's tapestry the indestructible threads of compassion, creativity, intuition, wisdom, and mutual respect. After reassessing the pluses to be found within a sisterhood, I reapplied for full membership into that communion of saintly women ... and was accepted.

Men

While this book documents a female navigator's solo expedition through the choppy seas of midlife crisis, I believe that the sons of our patriarchal culture must "come of age" by following much the same route. Like society's Superwomen, most men have ingested and digested misperceptions about what it means to be a "real" man or a "real" woman. As a result, members of both sexes perceive reality much as moles do; that is, they are blind to what is underneath their own noses. The fact that the masculine and feminine aspects within their own personalities are out of balance often eludes them. For many, the transition into midlife represents a rite of passage during which time full vision can be restored to women and men alike.

Over the course of my development, my view of men has moved through these stages: men as affectionate heroes; men as powerful predators; men as mentors of success; men as abusive traitors; men as wounded adults; and men as authentic adults. As a child, I saw my father as being the primary source of affection. Because he was generous with hugs and kisses, I tried hard to please him and to fulfill the unspoken expectations associated with being his "kitten." In adolescence, I felt that those same fatherly demonstrations of affection had begun to encroach upon my budding sense of sexuality. I recall that they often made me feel uncomfortable. At that same time, the strict voices of both church and parents warned me about the formidable consequences of being seduced by a date's devilish motives. As a teenager, the unconscious fear that I had begun to feel toward men surfaced repeatedly in dreams of abandonment, battering, stalking, and even murder.

During my years of young adulthood, the relationship with men in which I felt most comfortable was one of mentorship. Like Shaw's fictional Liza Doolittle, I discovered my personalized version of Professor Higgins while I was at the University of Minnesota. Being mesmerized by this mentor, I allowed him to transform me into his Pygmalian perception of feminine knowledge, beauty, and refinement. As the music in our duet began to sour, so did my perception of men. I began to view them as being opportunistic traitors, betrayers of women, and abusers of power. Repeatedly, I witnessed them denying their driving rigidity and unreasonable demands. Taught to demean not only a woman's feminine talents, but also to distance themselves from the female side of their own personalities, men began to represent "bad medicine" in my mind. That notion changed radically when I met and married an "evolved energy system"; that is, a male who understood and respected both his masculine and feminine sides. A few years after my husband's death, I tip-toed back into the singles scene. It was within the context of a toxic relationship that I found one of my life's greatest teachers. The emotional trauma that I suffered as a result of that liaison turned out to contain the gift of grace. It heralded the onset of my Re-Membering rite of passage.

Because of therapy's healing effect, my embittered feelings toward men underwent yet another major change. I began to view them more as being wounded adults. I came to understand that, like those of women, the minds and hearts of men had been imprisoned under the harsh regime of patriarchy. That system has demanded much from its "little buddies." Unlike their female counterparts, most young boys who are forming their masculine identities need to separate themselves from the images modeled by their mothers. Instead, they look to adult males in order to figure out what masculinity is all about. Because grandfathers, fathers, brothers, and uncles have all been fragmented by patriarchal biases, few healthy and whole role models exist. For centuries, our society has expected boys to disavow their original balanced nature, to feel ashamed of the feminine parts of their psyches, and to nurture only the masculine force within themselves, even should it surface as combative, controlling, or destructive behavior.

While writing this book, I have had the good fortune of meeting a few males whose sense of self has evolved significantly at midlife. In trying to formulate their own definition of masculinity, those men confront their past with courage, live in their present with honesty, and contemplate their future with serenity and hope. I consider such men to be "soul-brothers." Like me, they are walking the spiral path that takes them back to their core identity. During that quest, they will need to descend deep into themselves, to purge their patriarchal demons, to embrace their indwelling feminine force, and to Re-Member the identity that will serve them well through middle age and beyond. I hope that I might experience a committed, intimate relationship with just such a seeker. Only Re-Membered men and Re-Membered women will be able to bring the gift of wholeness into an intimate relationship. By recognizing and by celebrating the divinity that lies within a balanced sense of self, these authentic human beings will be able to love themselves, respect each other, teach their children, and honor their planetary home.

THE RE-MEMBERING PROCESS AND MY RELATIONSHIP TO NATURE

Living my childhood, adolescence, and young adulthood as a "city mouse," I have only a few memories of my pre-midlife relationship to Mother Nature. In the summertime, I found it fun to lie on earth's grass-covered belly and to watch the clouds create animated images. During the late fall, I enjoyed seeing troupes of multi-colored leaves dance to their death in wind-swept ballets. Because Minnesota's frozen fingers would wrap around me early in the season and would keep me chilled to the bone until spring, I spent most of the those months in hibernation. Enticed outside by springtime's wake-up calls, I took delight in the sounds and the smells of new life.

Reflection has shown me that I began to redefine my connection to Mother Nature sometime in my thirties. Until then, I had "tuned out" her feminine whispers and "tuned up" the masculine voice of reason. Once I had split away from the female principle within myself, l was more ready than ever to accept this hierarchical "chain of submission" as being valid: God, Angels, Men, Women, Children, Animals, Plants, and Minerals. Not until depression gnawed away my ego-inflated exterior did my inner core begin to acknowledge its sacred, yet humble, relationship to the Mother Earth.

As I explored Greek myths and rituals for this book, I discovered that in the beginning was Gaia, the primordial earth goddess. In my heart and my history, she carries the name Mother Nature. Gaia, meaning "rich in gifts" or "all giving" was the mother and grandmother to both goddesses and gods. Christine Downing states: "Gaia is mother of the beginning ...

(she) is earth made invisible, earth become metaphor, earth as realm of the soul .... There is a with-in-ness to Gaia; souls live in her body. The Greeks understood that soul-making happens in earth, not in sky .... Although she is there from the beginning, our discovery of Gaia is always a return, a re-cognition."[19]

During my Re-Membering rite of passage, I found my soul in Gaia's divine realm. For over a year, I tried literally to connect with her on a daily basis. During that imaginative time, I rested in Mother Nature's arms, cried on her shoulder, sat on her lap, told her my fears, and learned from her other "children." By "giving her all" to me, Gaia, in the role of Mother Nature, breathed life back into my feminine psyche. As a result of a most intimate relationship with both Mother Nature and Father God, I experienced my second birth as a Re-Membered Adultwoman.

THE RE-MEMBERING PROCESS AND MY RELATIONSHIP TO GOD

Throughout most of my childhood, the concept that I had of God closely resembled the image that had graced the cover of my Baltimore Catechism. I likened God to a mystical male authority figure who existed in Oz-like ethers "somewhere over the rainbow." I wanted to be His child and to believe that He loved me in spite of myself. In time, my adolescent attitudes toward mortal men began to affect my relationship to God. As I grew more afraid of His anger, my fear made His love for me feel more "iffy."

That image of God was one thing I left behind as I blossomed into young adulthood. God no longer existed in my mind as an omnipresent, omnipotent, omniscient anthropomorphized figure. Instead, God was, is, and always would be an unfathomable energy source with whom I was connected via the Holy Spirit. As a Christian, I believed that The Word had become flesh and had dwelled among us. Jesus became my model of love incarnate and of wholeness. I realized that, as The Christ, Jesus expressed dimensions of both the masculine and the feminine sides of His human nature. Refusing to succumb to the gender biases inherent in the patriarchal society of His day, Jesus never split away from the divine wholeness that indwelled Him; that is, He remained true to His True Self. In early adulthood, I began to react to the invisible profile that had been foisted upon Roman Catholic women by members of the patriarchal hierarchy. Because my mind and my heart abhorred its obvious biases and ingrained imbalances, organized religion became an anathema to my spiritual integrity. I stopped going to church. Instead, I became familiar with the basic tenets that underlie Judaism, Buddhism, Hinduism, Islam, and Native American spirituality. I became a practitioner of yoga, explored various types of meditation, and clarified my concept of God through my reconnection with nature.

As I approached midlife, the crises associated with death, depression, emotional pain, and physical collapse became raw materials for a spiritual renaissance. By relinquishing my ego-engendered sense of "i," I created the void that eventually was filled by the spiritual sense of "I AM." During the Re-Membering rite, my relationship to God matured. We became co-designers of a new authentic identity. God became The Potter and I, claiming my close connection to Mother Earth, willingly became the clay. Janice Brewi and Anne Brennan add these ideas to their description of midlife's remolding process: "The 'clay' is not merely passive; it has freedom enough to dare to resist the work of the Potter while in reality its freedom is not for such resistance, but for co-creation .... The artist knows his clay. He has a feel for its every movement. He knows his own ... vision and how to urge the ever-changing and often deviant process toward that vision."[20] I know that God's vision of me has always been one of wholeness. My vision of God has become one of divine balance: the sacred male and the sacred female.

As a Re-Membered woman, I realize that my relationship to God is dictated not from a source outside of myself but from deep within me. God's androgynous face shines upon me and reflects in my awareness that to be truly human is to be totally whole. I use a yoga exercise or "asana" called the Sun Salutation to close my morning meditation. I repeat that exercise four times, once in each geographical direction. That act deepens my understanding of the wholistic nature of God that permeates all of creation. Facing East, I acknowledge the presence of God, the Father in my life. As I stand looking into the South, I express my gratitude to God, the Child. When I turn toward the West, I give thanks to God, the Mother. Finally, I acknowledge the presence of God, the Holy Spirit as I face toward the North. No longer am I a child of God. In the process of Re-Membering, I became an adult of God. From that perspective, my relationship to an Omnipresent Power resembles the one I have with my breath: an invisible, internal life-giving force that urges me to expand outside of my own borders into my true potential.

SUMMARY

As one of society's Synthetic Superwomen of the seventies and the eighties, I exhibited mastery of academic, business, and social competencies that were designed to make me a "winner" in the world outside myself. While developing that consciousness, I established patterns of relating to myself as well as to other people and to important concepts in my life. Those patterns served me well for over two decades. Then, sometime in my late thirties, voices from an inner world confronted me with this earth-shattering realization: most of my life's story was a myth. It was a dream that spawned an identity as well as relationships that were based upon illusions. The voices taunted me with this question: "Who are you ... really?" Heeding their prodding to go inward, I experienced the demise and the decomposition of my phantom self. The long, painful, and sometimes frightening process of Re-Membering led me to a new and a more intimate level of consciousness about myself and my relationship to others. When I began to embrace the True Self that had been within me since my beginning, I started to understand the mystical and harmonious union that is meant to exist between me and all of God's creation. The expression, *Namaste,*[21] is an honorific greeting used throughout various regions of the Himalayas that means, "I behold the divine in you." I use it now to describe how I relate to myself and to others as a Re-Membered woman, an Authentic Adultwoman of God.

CONCLUSION

The Mid-Life transition is the time of gestation—not nine months—but close to seven or nine years. It is a bridge into the journey of the self. It is a bridge into the coming-home period of our lives.

Janice Brewi & Anne Brennan
Mid-Life

I STEPPED ONTO THE SPIRAL bridge of midlife Re-Membering soon after my husband's death in March, 1983. This dream's voice says to me, "It's time to step off. You've made it across. Welcome home!"

Journal Entry: November 11, 1992 3:13 A.M.

Although I feel strangely calm, I have to write about my dream.

I am standing all alone in my childhood bedroom. Everything is tidy and the two single beds are made. There is a beautiful white cat curled up on my pillow. I walk over to her and reach out to pet her. With that gesture, the cat's head enlarges several times, and she leaps angrily in my direction. Frightened, I run toward the closed bedroom door. A tall serene woman opens it from the outside. She helps me to escape.

Together, we walk down a long corridor. It brings us to the kitchen of my childhood home. We stand at the back door gazing out from its window. I see several picnic tables set up in the distance. They seem to be piled high with food, primarily fruit of all kinds. I know that one of those tables is to be my destination. However, between my home and the tables is an enormous field. Whatever has been planted in it has been covered with a couple of feet of fresh manure. The woman looks at the field, then at my bare feet. "Go ahead," she whispers.

As soon as I open the kitchen door, I begin to arrange the skirt of my pale pink sundress. I am worried about soiling it. I sink into the manure and begin to plod forward. The smell and the sensation nearly overwhelm me. The woman keeps calling to me from her post at the kitchen door, "Keep your head up and your eyes open."

I continue to wade through the muck. When able to see the edge of the field, I notice that there is only one elderly man sitting at the most distant table. He is wearing a monk's robe and sandals. As I step out of the field onto dry land, I am no longer wearing my sundress, rather I have on a full-length white slip. Everything about me is clean—even my feet. The man motions to me to join him. Feeling unafraid, I respond immediately. Taking a seat to his right, I sense that I am being devoured by his sky-blue eyes and massaged by his gentle nature. He points to an infected boil on my left elbow that resembles a tennis ball. As he touches it, the boil bursts. I watch as a mixture of blood, water, and pus pours out. After that painless cleansing, my elbow looks normal; that is, there is no trace of a scab or a scar. Without speaking, he conveys this message to me telepathically, "I am your friend and you are loved."

Just as everyone dreams, everyone has a story to tell. That dream summarizes my soul's story at midlife: a journey of trudging fully conscious through a field covered with manure, of witnessing the death and the burial of my Superwoman identity somewhere in those "mounds of *mierda*," of meeting the Suppressed Shrew as well as the Wise Woman within myself, of finding the compassionate male part of my psyche, and, finally, of Re-Membering myself into a balanced, mature Authentic Adultwoman. I have emerged Phoenix-like from the Re-Membering rite with a woman's body, an adult's mind, a child's heart, and a mystic's soul. With that perspective, I felt compelled to pursue my "survivor's mission": to generate a guidebook through midlife transition for my sister pilgrims. As a transpersonal teacher, I have drawn heavily from the feminine realms of creativity, intuition, imagination, and nature. In the role of transitional guide, I have acknowledged, from the outset, the uniqueness that each initiate brings to her midlife rite of passage. While the five stages provide a general roadmap through virgin territory, each woman must individualize her own itinerary based upon her personal history, her temperament, her timeframe, her support system, and her choices.

The Re-Membering model of midlife transition was a generative but disruptive process that caused me to live in "suspended time." Like bolts of lightning, ancient voices sliced through the dark thunderous clouds of depression that engulfed me, and they struck my inner core. They challenged me to reclaim my inherent birthright of wholeness by crossing the Re-Membering bridge. While maneuvering from one end to the other, I mastered many difficult tasks: to reconcile past losses; to comprehend my feminine psyche; to surrender my Superwoman identity; to gestate an adult sense of self; and to reclaim my authenticity. As I moved through the initiation rite, I discovered the knowledge and acquired the ability to transmute a variety of feelings and behaviors. I became able to change fear into strength, complexity into simplicity, fragmentation into unity, darkness into light, imbalance into balance, anxiety into serenity, sadness into joy, and, self-loathing into self-love. Because I consider each of those transmutations to be a grace-filled gift, I take none of them for granted.

Answering Superwomen's Questions

Since a major reason for writing *SuperWoman's Rite of Passage* was to help other high-achieving women negotiate their transitions into middle age, I have decided to address and to answer some questions that were posed to me by readers during the writing process.

Question: What are some symptoms that midlife Re-Membering is underway?

Re-Membering happens when a woman's body, mind, and spirit communicate this message frequently and clearly: your youthful gods of yesterday are about to be dethroned. Physically, her bionic energy begins to wane. While once able to juggle several projects simultaneously, Superwoman discovers that she must prioritize them and concentrate fully on only one or two of them at a time. It may feel as if she has lost control of her bustline, her waistline, and her "bottom line." She finds herself humming the tune, "I Can't Get No Satisfaction" in the boardroom, behind the steering wheel, over the counter, in the pew, as well as under the sheets. Lethargy, discontent, confusion, fatigue, boredom, anger, and procrastination are a few harbingers of midlife transition. Perhaps Re-Membering's most obvious symptoms are encapsulated in these questions: "Who am I?" and "Why am I here?"

Question: Why is midlife a crisis?

Midlife is touted to be a crisis because that is its nature. In my dictionary, one definition of "crisis" is "an emotionally significant event or a radical change of status in a person's life."[1] Midlife is "an anxiety-producing gap in the life cycle"[2] that pushes both men and women over an invisible threshold and into the second half of their lives. Midlife demands that we assume the status of authentic adults, a role which most of us are quite unprepared to understand or unwilling to assume. Midlife represents a major decision point in the flowchart of adult life. The crisis comes because of the question posed at that decision point: Should I move ahead or stay where I am? If I choose to stay put, I stagnate by clinging to yesterday's dreams and expectations. If I decide to proceed, I expand my self-awareness by reconciling past wounds, confronting inner demons, accommodating changes in relationships, and shedding the skin that encased my former sense of identity. Choosing to move ahead at midlife requires the adult to ask and to answer prickly but profound questions. Some of them are listed below:

> Should I redirect my focus from outside myself to inside myself?
>
> Should I withdraw from my familiar sense of identity to embrace my True Self?
>
> Should I decide to grow or to stagnate?
>
> Should I reconcile or hang on to past wounds and resentments?
>
> Should I embrace or reject my human limitations and failings?
>
> Should I speak in my own voice or echo the voices of others?
>
> Should I accept or deny my mortality?

Those questions and their answers reinforce society's tendency to relate midlife to mayhem. Asking such types of questions and answering them is bound to bring about change. While the Chinese character for the concept of change includes both the symbol for crisis and for opportunity, change connotes only crisis in the minds of many North American adults. There is yet another culture-bound explanation for this negative association.

Western society, especially that of North America, commends youth and condemns age. In spite of advanced degrees and practical life experience, many young adults believe that maybe life, but for certain most of its pleasurable perks, will end at forty. Increased education and research into this much-ignored developmental cycle of adult life will normalize it and will smooth out some of its "wrinkles."

Question: How would you support a woman who is Re-Membering herself?

There are many direct and indirect ways to offer support to a woman who is moving through the Re-Membering rite of passage. I present the following suggestions in a way that will be easy to recall:

R REFRAME the idea of midlife by stressing the growth-producing aspects.

E EXPLORE past losses with her as well as her patterns of grieving.

M MINIMIZE your advice giving.

E EMPHASIZE the need to express all feelings honestly.

M MAKE LISTS of her strengths, talents, accomplishments.

B BE honest.

E ENCOURAGE the practice of solitude and simplicity.

R READ books and articles about midlife change.

I IDENTIFY appropriate support networks.

N NURTURE with nature.

G GET PROFESSIONAL INTERVENTION, if necessary.

Question: Did you find yourself in more than one stage at a time?

I moved sequentially through the stages of the Re-Membering rite of passage. In proceeding that way, I focused my attention on the tasks associated with a specific stage which I called my "base." Although I was not able to skip over an entire stage, I recall experiencing behavioral and emotional "flashbacks" and "fast forwards." During those fleeting episodes, I would slip back or slide forward and identify with a feeling or a behavior that characterized a stage in the model other than my base stage. Because of their impermanence, those experiences were especially disorienting and frustrating for me. Explanations for them might include a) the Re-Membering model is a cyclical, not linear one; and, b) my identity consists of several subpersonalities, each of which might be Re-Membered within different timeframes.

Question: What stage was the most challenging to your relationships?

I became acutely aware of increased strain within my relationships when I was "based" in Stages I and III. While I was identifying and reconciling wounds from my past, people, especially those who were very close to me, began to detect my pain and my disillusionment. The clarity of well-established patterns of interaction blurred. As uncertainty became the norm, both they and I felt increased levels of discomfort. During Stage III, depression assaulted me head-on. I felt compelled to withdraw physically and emotionally from family members, friends, and colleagues. I yearned to isolate myself in the security of solitude. Several long-standing relationships "died" while I was in the third stage of Re-Membering myself.

Question: What happens to women after Stage V?

Once an initiate has Re-Membered herself, she will most likely experience a highly generative second half of life; that is, one of continuous learning and growth. Feeling at home with simplicity, solitude, service, and spirituality, the mature woman will affirm her authenticity by recognizing her connection to all things of God. While fearing neither life nor death, she will design a lifestyle characterized by balance. She will listen to the voice within a smile or a tear, and will check in regularly with her mother, Nature. I do not want to imply that a Re-Membered woman will sail through the second half of her life without problems. On the contrary, there will be obstacles and detours. Having rediscovered her inner core, however, the mature woman will be able to perceive them from a position of power and will negotiate them with confidence.

Question: How do you know when you have moved through a stage?

Upon reflection, I depended upon my intuition to tell me when I was ready to progress from one stage of the process to another. Some inner voice tutored me about what lessons I had to learn, then told me when I had mastered them.

Question: Must all women Re-Member themselves?

In order to "age successfully,"[3] both women and men need to Re-Member themselves at midlife. The primary challenge at this pivotal time is twofold: 1) to relinquish the "i" of the theoretical self created during the morning of one's life; and 2) to rediscover the "I" of the True Self in order to live life's afternoon and evening segments authentically.

Question: Can you elaborate on why rituals are important?

The word "ritual" describes "a system of rites or a ceremonial act."[4] Although members of North America's dominant culture experience relatively few rituals, such secular and religious rites have been a part of human existence since ancient times. Artifacts from those periods indicate that the feminine was revered as being the creative source of life. Seasonal, sexual, spiritual, familial, and life cycle rituals were enacted throughout the world around that theme. While women have been the customary markers of such changes, few contemporary rituals exist that either reflect or celebrate aspects of their feminine nature. Women need rituals in order to Re-Member their historical significance.

Imber-Black and Roberts state: "rituals embrace continuity and change."[5] They create a context in which a woman is able to relate to her past, present, and future. Rituals are agents of change. They provide a format for the symbolic marking of growth, movement, relationship, healing, and faith. Encouraging a woman to draw upon her feminine gifts of creativity and of imagination, rituals give personal meaning to her beliefs, feelings, values, and relationships without depending upon words. When familiar objects become sacred symbols, a woman can ease her transition into an unknown domain in a way that is practical and mystical.

Question: Did anything positive happen to you as Superwoman?

For well over two decades, I felt comfortable with and proud of my Superwoman identity. I had been tenacious in honing the skills that I thought were necessary to experience success in a man's world. As Superwoman, I epitomized independence, courage, responsibility, objectivity, risk-taking, and linear thinking. Those male-oriented qualities brought me a variety of rewards including financial remuneration, professional recognition, and personal satisfaction. Wearing that suit of armor, I completed a doctorate degree, started two businesses, lived and worked abroad, bought and sold two homes, got married, and had a child. Those were all wonderful events in my life. Although the male and female aspects of my Superwoman's psyche were unbalanced, she had encouraged me to acquire both the "book knowledge" and the "street wisdom" needed to identify and manage the overwhelming challenges associated with this profile: young widow/single parent.

Question: Why did you confine yourself to Greek goddesses?

One of the first books on goddess mythology that I read was Jean Shinoda Bolen's work, *Goddesses in Everywoman.* Enchanted by the archetypal figures described in that text, I decided to call a few of them "Mythic Mentors" and to integrate them into the Re-Membering model as well as into my daily life.

Question: Is the Re-Membering model of transition culture-bound?

Within the first part of *SuperWoman's Rite of Passage,* I emphasized the fact that the Re-Membering model of midlife transition documented an autobiographical journey; therefore, the construct as well as the content needs to be interpreted within that context. I used personal reflection to design the model and drew supporting material from literature published in the fields of psychology, mythology, and feminist spirituality. The primary targeted population for this work includes highly-educated, highly-motivated, white, middle-class women between the ages of thirty-five and fifty. It may be that the stages are applicable to broader populations of midlife women; however, generalizability is limited by factors that include ethnic, racial, educational, economic, and social backgrounds.

Question: Why did it take you so long to Re-Member yourself?

I needed nine years to move through the Re-Membering rite of passage. While not a student of numerology, I have been told that the number nine represents the concept of completion. Initially, my denial surrounding childhood losses, spousal death, emotional battering, and physical burnout extended the length of time I needed to move through the initiation process. Also, responsibilities associated with single parenting and business ownership influenced my progression. It took me almost three years to peel away the thin-skinned layers of my "identity onion." As I moved down into the juicier rings, depression took hold of me, and I became stuck. At that point, professional intervention supported and guided me. Each initiate must establish her own pace through the rite of passage. At the end, there is no gold medal presented for speed. On the contrary, thoroughness is its own reward. It took me almost a decade to experience the mysteries associated with death, pregnancy, and birth at midlife. I have no regrets!

While composing these final paragraphs, I feel myself inserting twinges of apprehension and of sadness into each space that separates the words. For the past two years, my focus has been well defined: to untangle and to write about the crisis of midlife transition. My journey through that anticipated time brought me face-to-face with a part of my feminine nature that I had forfeited decades ago. Thousands of years earlier, Western culture had exiled that same powerful source of energy to the darkness of the underworld. Like a hibernating she-bear, female energy has lain dormant deep within the womb of the earth. Now, as this millenium ends, that energy has begun to tremble in anticipation of a new and vital incarnation. As a Re-Membered adult, I intend to stay directly connected to that womanly wellspring as I write the second half of my human story.

According to Vicki Noble, "Once a woman has done the work of re-membering herself, she is much more able to change the world effectively."[6] It is we, both women and men at midlife's juncture, who must stretch into our REAL potential as Re-Membered agents of change. In that context, what do I mean by "real"? I found my definition of that word in a children's picture book, *The Velveteen Rabbit.* Little rabbit asked the playroom veteran, Skin Horse, to define the word "real" and to tell if being real hurts.

> "Sometimes," said the Skin Horse, for he was always truthful, "when you are REAL you don't mind being hurt."
>
> "Does it happen all at once, like being wound up," he asked "or bit by bit?"
>
> "It doesn't happen all at once," said the Skin Horse. "You become. It takes a long time. That's why it doesn't often happen to people who break easily or have sharp edges, or who have to be carefully kept. Generally, by the time you are REAL, most of your hair has been loved off, and your eyes drop out and you get loose in the joints and very shabby. But these things don't matter at all, because once you are REAL, you can't be ugly, except to people who don't understand."[7]

The Re-Membering rite of passage is about becoming REAL. Because it requires a Superwoman to break down illusions, to file down sharp edges, and to grieve a variety of losses, midlife transition can unfold slowly and may hurt a lot. A Re-Membered woman is a REAL agent of change. In walking the spiral path, she has acquired first-hand knowledge of authenticity, integrity, interconnectedness, spirituality, and self-love. Societies need to seed themselves with REAL people—our global home demands it, our future generations deserve it and our eternal souls divine it.

If, during the course of your Re-Membering journey or after your coming-home celebration, you wish to ask me additional questions, to share your stories, to disagree with my observations, or to provide me with new insights, I invite you to write to me.

Know that I honor the invisible connection that exists between author and reader. In that spirit of interdependency, I wish you "Goddess-speed" on your soul-making journey through midlife and beyond. Blessings!

END NOTES

PREFACE

1. Marti Glenn, "Feeling the Inner Fire," *Venus Rising* 3, 1 (1989), p. 23.

2. Susan Faludi, *Backlash: The Undeclared War Against American Women* (New York: Crown Publishers, Inc., 1991).

3. Emily Hancock, *The Girl Within* (New York: Ballentine Books, 1989).

4. Ruthellen Josselson, *Finding Herself: Pathways to Identity Development in Women* (San Francisco: Jossey-Bass Publishers, 1987).

5. Maureen Murdock, *The Heroine's Journey* (Boston: Shambala Publishers, Inc., 1990).

6. Vicki Noble, *Shakti Woman* (San Francisco: Harper, 1991).

7. Polly Young-Eisendrath and Florence Weidemann, *Female Authority: Empowering Women Through Psychotherapy* (New York: The Guilford Press, 1987).

8. Ibid., p. 8.

9. Mathew Fox, *The Original Blessing* (Santa Fe, NM: Bear & Company, 1983), p. 10.

INTRODUCTION

Nor Hall, *The Moon and the Virgin.* (New York: HarperCollins, 1994), p. 38.

1. Jacquelyn Small, *Transformers: The Therapists of the Future* (Marina del Rey, CA: Devorss and Company, Publishing, 1982), p. 3

2. Mathew Fox, *Breakthrough: Meister Ekhart's Creation Spirituality in New Translation* (New York: Doubleday, 1980), p. 222.

PART I

William Patterson, *Eating the "I"* (San Anselmo, CA: Arete Communications, 1992), p. 26.

1. Alla Renée Bozarth, *At the Foot of the Mountain: Discovering Images for Emotional Healing* (Alla Reneé Bozarth, 1990), p. 128.
2. Hancock, *The Girl Within*, p. 3.
3. Hannah Hurnard, *Winds' Feet on High Places* (Wheaton, IL: Tynsdale House Publishing, Inc., 1977).
4. Hancock, *The Girl Within.*
5. Alice Koller, *An Unknown Woman: A Journey to Self-Discovery* (New York: Bantam Books, 1982).
6. Young-Eisendrath and Weidemann, *Female Authority,* pp. 1–2.
7. Murdock, *The Heroine's Journey,* p. 17.
8. Mary Catherine Bateson, *Composing a Life* (New York: Penguin Books, 1989).
9. William Bridges, *Transitions: Making Sense of Life's Changes* (Reading, MA: Addison-Wesley, 1980).
10. Elisabeth Kubler-Ross, *Death: The Final Stage of Growth* (Englewood Cliffs, NJ: Prentice-Hall, 1975).
11. Carol Gilligan, *In a Different Voice: Psychological Theory and Women's Development* (Cambridge, MA: Harvard University Press, 1982).
12. Jean Baker Miller, *Toward a New Psychology of Women* (Boston: Beacon Press, 1976).
13. Lillian Ribin, *Women of a Certain Age: The Midlife Search for Self* (New York: Harper & Row, 1979).
14. Gail Sheehy, *Passages: Predictable Crises in Adult Life* (New York: E. P. Dutton Company, 1974).
15. Bozarth, *At the Foot of the Mountain*, p. 128.

16. Lesley Shore, *Healing the Feminine: Reclaiming Woman's Voice* (St. Paul, MN: Llewellyn Publications, 1992).

17. Patterson, *Eating the "I"*, p. 337.

18. Jean Shinoda Bolen, *Goddesses In Everywoman* (New York: Harper & Row, Publishers, 1984).

19. Patterson, *Eating the "I"*, p. 92.

20. Kathleen Fischer, *Women at the Well: Feminine Perspectives on Spiritual Development* (New York: Paulist Press, 1988).

PART II

Stage I: The Wounds

Sheehy, *Passages: Predictable Crises in Adult Life* (New York: E. P. Dutton Company, 1974), p. 319.

1. Alla Renée Bozarth, *Life is Goodbye/Life is Hello: Grieving Well Through All Kinds of Loss*, revised edition (Center City, MN: Hazelden, 1986), p. 99.

2. Bolen, *Goddesses in Everywoman*, p. 197.

3. Karl Kerenyi, *Gods of the Greeks* (Great Britain: Billings and Sons, 1951, Reprinted, 1982), p. 132.

4. Mark Morford and Robert Lenardon, *Classical Mythology*, Second Edition (New York: Longman Publishing Company, 1977), p. 231.

5. Bolen, *Goddesses in Everywoman*, p. 197.

6. Kerenyi, *Gods of the Greeks*, p. 244.

7. Morford and Lenardon, p. 241.

8. Bolen, *Goddesses in Everywoman*, p. 132.

9. Kerenyi, *Gods of the Greeks*, p. 199.

10. Ibid., p. 202.

11. Ibid., p. 197.

12. Hancock, *The Girl Within*, p. 22.

13. Ibid., p. 25.
14. Ibid., p. 34.
15. Young-Eisendrath and Weidemann, *Female Authority,* p. 2.
16. Lucia Cappacchione, *The Creative Journal* (North Hollywood, CA: Newcastle Publications, 1989).
17. Janet Hagberg and Richard Leider, *The Inventurers: Excursions in Life Career Renewal* (Reading, MA: Addison-Wesley Publishing Co., 1982).
18. Murdock, *The Heroine's Journey.*
19. Gilligan, *In a Different Voice.*
20. Sherry Ruth Anderson and Patricia Hopkins, *The Feminine Face of God* (New York: Bantam Books, 1991).
21. Shirley Nicholson, *The Goddess Re-Awakening* (Wheaton, IL: The Theosophical Publishing House, 1989).
22. Bozarth, *At The Foot of the Mountain,* p. 182.
23. Dr. Herbert Freudenberger and Gail North, *Women's Burnout: How to Spot It, How to Reverse It, & How to Prevent It* (New York: Penguin Books, 1986), p. 76.
24. Ibid., p. 75.

Stage II: The Dying

Stephen Levine, *Meetings At the Edge* (New York: Anchor Press, 1984), p. 106.

1. Anderson and Hopkins, *The Feminine Face of God,* p. 49.
2. Josselson, *Finding Herself,* p. 178.
3. Bolen, *Goddesses in Everywoman,* pp. 174–175.
4. Kerenyi, *Gods of the Greeks,* p. 233.
5. Bolen, *Goddesses in Everywoman,* p. 132.
6. Kerenyi in Christine Downing, *The Goddess: Mythological Images of the Feminine* (New York: Crossroad Publishing, 1990), p. 40.

7. Bozarth, *Life is Goodbye/Life is Hello*, pp. 99–100.

8. Bolen, *Goddesses in Everywoman*, p. 174.

9. Jaquelyn Small, *Transformers: The Therapist of the Future*

10. Morford and Lenardon, *Classical Mythology*, p. 218.

11. *Websters Seventh Collegiate Dictionary*, p. 580.

12. Small, *Transformers*, p. 216.

Stage III: The Dying

Koller, *An Unknown Woman*, p. 110.

1. Kerenyi, *The Gods of the Greeks*, p. 91.

2. Bolen, *Goddesses in Everywoman*, p. 108.

3. Morford and Lenardon, *Classical Mythology*, p. 60.

4. Bolen, *Goddesses in Everywoman*, p. 108.

5. Ibid., 224.

6. Kerenyi, *Gods of the Greeks*, p. 92.

7. "The Hymn to Aphrodite I," in *Homeric Hymns*, trans., Charles Boer, rev. ed. (Irving, TX: Spring, 1979), p. 70.

8. Bolen, *Goddesses in Everywoman*, p. 115.

9. Bridges, *Transitions*, p. 129.

10. *Webster's Seventh Collegiate Dictionary*, p. 1296.

11. Morford and Lenardon, *Classical Mythology*, p. 60.

12. Bolen, *Goddesses in Everywoman*, p. 117.

13. Murdock, *The Heroine's Journey*, p. 139.

14. Brother Lawrence, *The Practice of the Presence of God* (Old Tappen, NJ: Spire Books, 1958).

15. Bolen, *Goddesses in Everywoman*, p. 111.

16. Anderson and Hopkins, *The Feminine Face of God*, p. 209.

17. **Baldwin, *Life's Companion*.**

18. Carol Christ, *Diving Deep and Surfacing: Women Writers on a Spiritual Quest* (Boston: Beacon Press, 1980).

19. Meinrad Craighead, *The Mother's Songs: Images of God the Mother* (Mahway, NJ: Paulist Press, 1986).

20. Mary Giles, *The Feminist Mystic and Other Essays on Women and Spirituality* (New York: Crossroads Press, 1982).

21. Marsha Sinetar, *Ordinary People as Monks and Mystics: Lifestyles for Self-Discipline* (New York: Paulist Press, 1986).

22. May Sarton, *Journal of a Solitude* (New York: Norton, 1973).

23. Harriet Goldhor Lerner. *The Dance of Anger* (New York: Harper & Row, 1985), p. 20.

24. Ibid., p. 20.

25. Ibid., p. 20.

26. Ibid., p. 25.

27. Joyce Rupp, *The Star in My Heart* (San Diego: LuraMedia, 1990), p. xii.

28. Small, *Transformers*, p. 130.

Stage IV: The Gestation

Rainer Maria Rilke, *Letters to a Young Poet*, trans. by H. Norton. (New York: Norton, 1954), pp. 29–30.

1. Psalm 139.

2. Kerenyi, *Gods of the Greeks*, p. 41.

3. Downing, *The Goddess*, p. 165.

4. Morford and Lenardon, *Classical Mythology*, p. 151.

5. W. C. K. Guthrie, "The Greeks and Their Gods," in Downing, *The Goddess: Mythological Images of the Feminine* (New York: Crossroad Publishing Company, 1990), p. 164.

6. Bolen, *Goddesses in Everywoman*, p. 47.

7. Downing, *The Goddess*, pp. 157 and 159.

8. Morford and Lenardon, *Classical Mythology*, p. 112.

9. Downing, *The Goddess*, p. 165.

10. Ibid., p. 176.

11. Hancock, *The Girl Within*, p. 3.

12. Downing, *The Goddess: Mythological Images of the Feminine*, p. 175.

13. Kerenyi, *Gods of the Greeks*, p. 41.

14. Downing, *The Goddess: Mythological Images of the Feminine*, p. 159.

15. Clarissa Pinkola Estés, *Women Who Run With the Wolves: Myths & Stories of the Wild Woman Archetype* (New York: Random House, 1992), p. 27.

16. Ibid., p. 13.

17. Downing, *The Goddess: Mythological Images of the Feminine*, pp. 174–175.

18. Bolen, *Goddesses in Everywoman*, p. 53.

19. *Webster's Seventh Collegiate Dictionary*, p. 1021.

20. Bolen, *Goddesses in Everywoman*, p. 52.

21. Morford and Lenardon, *Classical Mythology*, p. 133.

22. Estés, *Women Who Run With the Wolves*, pp. 23–24.

23. Murdock, *The Heroine's Journey*, p. 93.

24. Ibid., p. 139.

25. Paula Hardin, *What are You Doing with the Rest of Your Life?* (San Rafael, CA: New World Library, 1992), p. 28.

Stage V: The Re-Birth

Murdock, *The Heroine's Journey*, p. 160.

1. Ann Keiffer, *Gift of the Dark Angel: A Woman's Journey Through Depression Toward Wholeness* (San Diego: LuraMedia, 1991), p. 1.

2. Kerenyi, *Gods of the Greeks*, p. 269.

3. Downing, *The Goddess*, p. 63.

4. Morford and Lenardon, *Classical Mythology*, p. 418.

5. Kerenyi, "Gods of the Greeks," in Young-Eisendrath and Weidemann, *Female Authority*, pp. 144–45.

6. Downing, *The Goddess*, p. 64.

7. Ibid., p. 63.

8. Kerenyi, "Dionysos," in Downing, *The Goddess*, p. 65.

9. Downing, *The Goddess*, p. 66.

10. Ibid., p. 64.

11. Ibid., p. 61.

12. Ibid., p. 63.

13. Ibid., pp. 64–65.

14. Ibid., p. 63.

15. Janice Brewi and Anne Brennan, *Mid-Life: Psychological and Spiritual Perspectives* (New York: Crossroad Publishing, 1991), p. 59.

PART III

Ann Morrow Lindbergh, *Gifts From the Sea* (New York: Pantheon Books, 1977), pp. 69–70.

1. *Webster's Seventh Collegiate Dictionary*, p. 723.

2. Young-Eisendrath and Weidemann, *Female Authority*, p. 8.

3. Murdock, *The Heroine's Journey*, p. 139.

4. Jamie Sams and David Carson, *Medicine Cards* (Santa Fe: Bear & Company, 1988), p. 210.

5. *Webster's Seventh New Collegiate Dictionary*, p. 732.

6. C. G. Jung in Janice Brewi and Anne Brennan, *Mid-Life: Psychological and Spiritual Perspectives*, p. 25.

7. Brewi and Brennan, *Mid-Life: Psychological and Spiritual Perspectives*, p. 21.
8. Sams and Carson, *Medicine Cards*, pp. 134–35.
9. Keiffer, *Gift of the Dark Angel* , p. 60.
10. Linda Budd, *Living With An Active Alert Child* (New York: Prentice Hall, 1990).
11. Jean Lanier, "Epigraph" in Sherry Ruth Anderson and Patricia Hopkins, *The Feminine Face of God*, p. 178.
12. Murdock, "Inner Man With a Heart," *The Heroine's Journey*, pp. 155–68.
13. *Webster's Seventh New Collegiate Dictionary*, p. 836.
14. Janice Brewi and Anne Brennan, *Celebrate Mid-Life: Jungian Archetypes and Mid-Life Spirituality* (New York: Crossroad Publishing, 1993), p. 55.
15. Jung, "Stages of Life," in *Modern Man in Search of a Soul*, in Hardin, *What Are You Doing With the Rest of Your Life?*, p. 77.
16. Brewi and Brennan, *Celebrate Mid-Life*, p. 54.
17. Maureen Murdock, "Healing the Mother/Daughter Split," in *The Heroine's Journey*, pp. 130–54.
18. Fischer, *Women at the Well*, p. 2.
19. Downing, "Beginning With Gaia," in *The Goddess*, pp.135 and 145.
20. Brewi, *Celebrate Mid-Life*, p. 67.
21. "Namaste."

CONCLUSION

Janice Brewi and Anne Brennan, *Celebrate Mid-Life*, p. 131.

1. *Webster's Seventh New Collegiate Dictionary*, p. 197.
2. Brewi and Brennan, *Mid-Life: Psychological and Spiritual Perspectives*, p. 25.

3. Hardin, *What Are You Doing With the Rest of Your Life?*, p. 25.

4. *Webster's Seventh New Collegiate Dictionary*, p. 743.

5. Evan Imber-Black and Jaime Roberts, *Rituals For Our Times* (New York: HarperCollins, 1986), p. 14.

6. Noble, *Shakti Woman*, p. 5.

7. Margery Williams, *The Velveteen Rabbit* (New York: Alfred A. Knopf, 1994), p. 12–14.

BIBLIOGRAPHY

Anderson, Sherry Ruth, and Patricia Hopkins. *The Feminine Face of God.* New York: Bantam Books, 1991.

Baldwin, Christina. *Life's Companion: Journal Writing as a Spiritual Quest.* New York: Bantam Books, 1990.

Bateson, Mary Catherine. *Composing a Life.* New York: Penguin Books, 1989.

Bolen, Jean Shinoda. *Goddesses in Everywoman.* New York: Harper & Row, 1984.

Bozarth, Alla. *At the Foot of the Mountain: Discovering Images for Emotional Healing.* Minneapolis, MN: CompCare Publishing Co., 1990.

__________. *Life is Goodbye/Life is Hello: Grieving Through All Kinds of Loss.* Center City, MN: Hazelden, 1986.

Brewi, Janice and Anne Brennan. *Celebrate Mid-Life: Jungian Archetypes and Mid-Life Spirituality.* New York: Crossroad Publishing, 1989.

Brewi, Janice, and Anne Brennan. *Mid-Life: Psychological and Spiritual Perspectives.* New York: Crossroad Publishing, 1991.

Bridges, William. *Transitions: Making Sense of Life's Changes.* Reading, MA: Addison-Wesley, 1980.

Brother Lawrence. *Practice of the Presence of God.* Garden City, NY: Image Books, 1977.

Budd, Linda S. *Living With the Active Alert Child.* New York: Prentice Hall, 1990.

Campbell, Joseph. *Myths To Live By.* New York: Bantam Books, 1973.

__________. "Joseph Campbell on the Great Goddess," *Parabola: Myth and the Quest for Meaning,* V(4) 1980, pp. 74–85.

Capacchione, Lucia. *The Creative Journal: The Art of Finding Yourself.* North Hollywood, CA: Newcastle Publications, 1989.

Carroll, L. Patrick, and Katherine M. Dykman. *Chaos or Creation: Spirituality in Mid-Life.* New York: Paulist Press, 1986.

Christ, Carol. *Diving Deep and Surfacing: Women Writers on Spiritual Quest.* Boston: Beacon Press, 1980.

Craighead, Meinrad. *The Mother's Songs: Images of God the Mother.* Mahwah, NJ: Paulist Press, 1986.

Downing, Christine. *The Goddess: Mythological Images of the Feminine.* New York: Crossroad Publishing Company, 1990.

Estés, Clarissa Pinkola. *Women Who Run With the Wolves: Myths & Stories of the Wild Woman Archetype.* New York: Random House, 1992.

Fahludi, Susan. *Backlash: The Undeclared War Against American Women.* New York: Crown Publishing, Inc., 1991.

Fischer, Kathleen. *Women at the Well: Feminine Perspectives on Spiritual Development.* New York: Paulist Press, 1988.

Fischer, L. R. *Linked Lives: Adult Daughters and Their Mothers.* New York: Harper & Row, 1987.

Fox, Mathew. *Breakthrough: Meister Ekhart's Creation Spirituality in New Translation.* New York: Doubleday, 1980.

__________. *The Original Blessing.* Santa Fe: Bear & Company, 1983.

Frankl, Viktor. *Man's Search For Meaning.* New York: Simon & Schuster, 1963.

Freudenberger, Dr. Herbert J., and Gail North. *Women's Burnout: How to Spot It, How to Reverse It, & How to Prevent It.* New York: Penguin Books, 1987.

Giles, Mary E. *The Feminist Mystic and Other Essays on Women and Spirituality.* New York: Crossroad Publishing Company, 1982.

Gilligan, Carol. *In A Different Voice: Psychological Theory and Women's Development.* Cambridge, MA: Harvard University Press, 1982.

Gimbutas, M. *The Language of the Goddess: Unearthing the Hidden Symbols of Western Civilization.* San Francisco: Harper & Row, 1989.

Glenn, Marti. "Feeling the Inner Fire," *Venus Rising*, 3, 1 (1989).

Gould, Roger. *Transformations: Growth and Change in Adult Life*. New York: Simon and Schuster, 1978.

Gray, Elizabeth D. (ed.) *Sacred Dimensions of Women's Experience*. Wellesley, MA: Roundtable Press, 1988.

Griffin, Susan. *Woman and Nature: The Roaring Inside Her*. New York: Harper & Row, 1978.

Guthrie, W. K. C. *Greeks and Their Gods*. Boston: Beacon Press, 1955.

Haddon, G. P. *Body Metaphors: Releasing the God-Feminine in Us All*. New York: Crossroad Publishing, 1988.

Hagberg, Janet, and Richard Leider. *The Inventurers: Excursions in Life Career Renewal*. Reading, MA: Addison-Wesley Publishing Co., 1982.

Hall, Nor. *The Moon and the Virgin*. New York: HarperCollins, 1994.

Hancock, Emily. *The Girl Within*. New York: Ballentine Books, 1989.

Hardin, Paula. *What Are You Doing With the Rest of Your Life?* San Rafael, CA: New World Library, 1992.

Harding, Ester. *Woman's Mysteries: Ancient and Modern*. New York: Bantam Books, 1973.

Hurnard, Hannah. *Winds' Feet on High Places*. Wheaton, IL: Tynsdale House Publishing, Inc., 1977.

Imber-Black, Evan, and Jaime Roberts. *Rituals For Our Times: Celebrating Healing and Changing Our Lives and Relationships*. New York: HarperCollins, 1986.

Josselson, Ruthellen. *Finding Herself: Pathways to Identity Development in Women*. San Francisco: Jossey-Bass, Inc., 1987.

Jung, Carl G. "Stages in Life," in *Modern Man in Search of a Soul*. Translated by W. S. Dell and Gary F. Baynes. New York: Harcourt Brace and World, 1933.

Keiffer, Ann. *Gift of the Dark Angel; A Woman's Journey Through Depression Toward Wholeness*. San Diego: LuraMedia, 1991.

Kerenyi, Karl. *Gods of the Greeks.* Great Britain: Billings and Sons, 1951. Reprinted, 1982.

Koller, Alice. *An Unknown Woman: A Journey to Self-Discovery.* New York: Bantam Books, 1981.

Kubler-Ross, Elisabeth. *Death: The Final Stage of Growth.* Englewood Cliffs, NJ: Prentice-Hall, 1975.

Larrington, Carolyne. *The Feminist Companion to Mythology.* San Francisco: Thorsons Publishing Company, 1992.

Lerner, Harriet Goldhor. *The Dance of Anger: A Woman's Guide to Changing the Patterns of Intimate Relationships.* New York: Harper & Row, 1985.

Levine, Stephen. *Meetings at the Edge: Conversations with the Grieving & the Dying, the Healing & the Healed.* New York: Anchor Press, 1984.

Lindbergh, Anne Morrow. *Gifts From the Sea.* New York: Pantheon Books, 1977.

Luke, Helen M. *Woman: Earth and Spirit.* New York: Crossroad Publishing, 1981.

Miller, Jean Baker. *Toward a New Psychology of Women.* Boston: Beacon Press, 1976.

Morford, Mark P. O., and Robert J. Lenardon. *Classical Mythology.* Second Edition. New York: Longman Publishing Company, 1977.

Murdock, Maureen. *The Heroine's Journey.* Boston: Shambala Publishing Inc., 1990.

Nicholson, Shirley. *The Goddess Reawakening.* Wheaton, IL: The Theosophical Publishing House, 1989.

Noble, Vicki. *Shakti Woman: Feeling Our Fire, Healing Our World.* San Francisco: Harper, 1991.

Patterson, William P. *Eating of the "I".* San Anselmo, CA: Arete Communication Publishing, Inc., 1992.

Perera, Sylvia Brinton. *Descent to the Goddess.* Toronto: Inner City Books, 1981.

Rich, Adrienne. *Of Woman Born: Motherhood as Experience and Institution.* New York: Bardam Books, 1976.

Rilke, Rainer Maria. *Letters to a Young Poet.* Translated by Stephen Mitchell. New York: Random House Books, 1986.

Rubin, Lillian B. *Women of a Certain Age: The Midlife Search for Self.* New York: Harper & Row, 1979.

Rupp, Joyce. *The Star in My Heart: Experiencing Sophia, Inner Wisdom.* San Diego: LuraMedia, 1990.

Sams, Jamie, and David Carson. *Medicine Cards: The Discovery of Power Through the Ways of Animals.* Santa Fe: Bear & Company, 1988.

Sarton, May. *Journal of a Solitude.* New York: W. W. Norton, 1973.

Schaef, Anne W. *Women's Reality: An Emerging Female System in a White Male Society.* Rev. Ed. San Francisco: Harper & Row, 1985.

Sheehy, Gail. *Passages: Predictable Crises in Adult Life.* New York: E. P. Dutton Company, 1974.

Shore, Lesley. *Healing the Feminine: Reclaiming Woman's Voice.* St Paul, MN: Llewellyn Publications, 1992.

Sinetar, Marsha. *Ordinary People as Monks and Mystics: Lifestyles for Self-Discovery.* New York: Paulist Press, 1986.

Small, Jacquelyn. *Transformers: The Therapists of the Future.* Marina del Rey, CA: DeVorss and Company Publishing, 1982.

Starhawk. *The Spiral Dance: A Rebirth of the Ancient Religion of the Great Goddess.* San Francisco: Harper & Row, 1979.

Stein, Diane. *The Goddess Celebrates: An Anthology of Women's Rituals.* Freedon, CA: The Crossing Press, 1991.

Stone, Merlin. *When God Was a Woman.* San Diego: Harcourt Brace Jovanovich, 1976.

VanGennep, Arnold. Trans. by Monika Vizedom and Gabrielle L. Caffee. *Rites of Passage.* Chicago: University of Chicago Press, 1960.

Walker, B. G. *The Crone: Women of Age, Wisdom, and Power.* San Francisco: Harper & Row, 1985.

Washbourn, Penelope. *Becoming Woman: The Quest for Spiritual Wholeness in Female Experience.* San Francisco: Harper & Row, 1977.

Webster's Seventh New Collegiate Dictionary. Springfield, MA: G & C Merriam Company, Publications, 1967.

Williams, Margery. *The Velveteen Rabbit: Or How Toys Become Real.* New York: Alfred A. Knopf, 1994.

Whitmont, Edward C. *Return of the Goddess.* New York: Crossroad Publishing, 1988.

Woodman, Marion. *The Pregnant Virgin: A Process of Psychological Transformation.* Toronto: Inner City Books, 1985.

Young-Eisendrath, Polly, and Florence Weidemann. *Female Authority: Empowering Women Through Psychotherapy.* New York: The Guilford Press, 1987.

INDEX

E

F

G

H

I

J

K

L

M

N

O

P

Q

R

S

STAY IN TOUCH!

On the following pages you will find listed, with their current prices, some of the books now available on related subjects. Your book dealer stocks most of these and will stock new titles in the Llewellyn series as they become available. We urge your patronage.

TO GET A FREE CATALOG

You are invited to write for our bimonthly news magazine/catalog, *Llewellyn's New Worlds of Mind and Spirit.* A sample copy is free, and it will continue coming to you at no cost as long as you are an active mail customer. Or you may subscribe for just $10 in the United States and Canada ($20 overseas, first class mail). Many bookstores also have *New Worlds* available to their customers. Ask for it.

In *New Worlds* you will find news and features about new books, tapes and services; announcements of meetings and seminars; helpful articles; author interviews and much more. Write to:

Llewellyn's New Worlds of Mind and Spirit
P.O. Box 64383-447, St. Paul, MN 55164-0383, U.S.A.

TO ORDER BOOKS AND TAPES

If your book store does not carry the titles described on the following pages, you may order them directly from Llewellyn by sending the full price in U.S. funds, plus postage and handling (see below).

Credit card orders: VISA, MasterCard, American Express are accepted. Call us toll-free within the United States and Canada at 1-800-THE-MOON.

Special Group Discount: Because there is a great deal of interest in group discussion and study of the subject matter of this book, we offer a 20% quantity discount to group leaders or agents. Our Special Quantity Price for a minimum order of five copies of *SuperWoman's Rite of Passage* is $59.80 cash-with-order. Include postage and handling charges noted below.

Postage and Handling: Include $4 postage and handling for orders $15 and under; $5 for orders over $15. There are no postage and handling charges for orders *over* $100. Postage and handling rates are subject to change. We ship UPS whenever possible within the continental United States; delivery is guaranteed. Please provide your street address as UPS does not deliver to P.O. boxes. Orders shipped to Alaska, Hawaii, Canada, Mexico and Puerto Rico will be sent via first class mail. Allow 4-6 weeks for delivery. International orders: **Airmail** – add retail price of each book and $5 for each non-book item (audiotapes, etc.); Surface mail – add $1 per item.

Minnesota residents add 7% sales tax.

Mail orders to:
Llewellyn Worldwide, P.O. Box 64383-447, St. Paul, MN 55164-0383, U.S.A.

For customer service, call (612) 291-1970.

Prices subject to change without notice.

THE BOOK OF GODDESSES & HEROINES
by Patricia Monaghan

The Book of Goddesses & Heroines is an historical landmark, a must for everyone interested in Goddesses and Goddess worship. It is not an effort to trivialize the beliefs of matriarchal cultures. It is not a collection of Goddess descriptions penned by biased male historians throughout the ages. It is the complete, non-biased account of Goddesses of every cultural and geographic area, including African, Egyptian, Japanese, Korean, Persian, Australian, Pacific, Latin American, British, Irish, Scottish, Welsh, Chinese, Greek, Icelandic, Italian, Finnish, German, Scandinavian, Indian, Tibetan, Mesopotamian, North American, Semitic and Slavic Goddesses!

Unlike some of the male historians before her, Patricia Monaghan eliminates as much bias as possible from her Goddess stories. Envisioning herself as a woman who might have revered each of these Goddesses, she has done away with language that referred to the deities in relation to their male counterparts, as well as with culturally relative terms such as "married" or "fertility cult." The beliefs of the cultures and the attributes of the Goddesses have been left intact.

Plus, this book has a new, complete index. If you are more concerned about finding a Goddess of war than you are a Goddess of a given country, this index will lead you to the right page. This is especially useful for anyone seeking to do Goddess rituals. Your work will be twice as efficient and effective with this detailed and easy-to-use book.

0-87542-573-9, 456 pp., 6 x 9, photos, softcover **$17.95**

HEALING THE FEMININE
Reclaiming Woman's Voice
by Lesley Irene Shore, Ph.D.
(formerly Reclaiming Woman's Voice)

Most self-help books for women inadvertently add to women's difficulties by offering ways to battle symptoms of distress without examining the underlying causes. One of the first of its kind, Healing the Feminine chronicles the struggles and triumphs of a psychologist and her clients on their personal journeys to self-discovery and wholeness.

Tracing much of women's distress to society's devaluation of the feminine, Dr. Shore illustrates the need for both men and women to reclaim their hidden but vital feminine aspects. Reconnecting with the feminine entails affirming the female experience, the female body, and the female way of being. Through a variety of methods that include breathing exercises, mental imagery, and living in tune with nature, we can learn to hear our hidden "Woman's Voice" and begin the journey to wholeness and peace.

1-56718-667-X, 208 pp., 5¼ x 8, softcover **$12.00**

Prices subject to change without notice.

DANCE OF POWER
A Shamanic Journey
by Dr. Susan Gregg

Join Dr. Susan Gregg on her fascinating, real-life journey to find her soul. This is the story of her shamanic apprenticeship with a man named Miguel, a Mexican-Indian Shaman, or "Nagual." As you live the author's personal experiences, you have the opportunity to take a quantum leap along the path toward personal freedom, toward finding your true self, and grasping the ultimate personal freedom—the freedom to choose moment by moment what you want to experience.

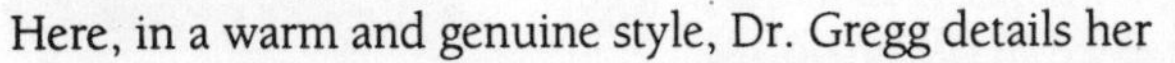

Here, in a warm and genuine style, Dr. Gregg details her studies with Miguel, her travel to other realms, and her initiations by fire and water into the life of a "warrior." If you want to understand how you create your own reality—and how you may be wasting energy by resisting change or trying to understand the unknowable—take the enlightening path of the Nagual. Practical exercises at the end of each chapter give you the tools to embark upon your own spiritual quest.

Learn about another way of being ... *Dance of Power* can change your life, if you let it.

0-87542-247-0, 240 pp.5¼ x 8, illus., photos, softbound **$12.95**

FINDING THE SACRED SELF
A Shamanic Workbook
by Dr. Susan Gregg

Imagine what your life would be like if you felt totally safe at all times ... loved unconditionally by all ... and passion filled your every moment. Sound impossible? Finding and living from your sacred self is a profound act that can change the world. But how do you grab onto that sacred self which is your essence?

This book is about Dr. Susan Gregg's own process of stopping her inner pain and reclaiming her essential self. In her first book, *The Dance of Power,* she described her apprenticeship with shamans Miguel and Sarita. Now, in *Finding Your Sacred Self,* she shares many of the exercises—which you can do alone or in a group—that helped her connect with her sacred self.

Through exercises such as "meeting your protector," "mirror meditations" and "channeling healing energies," you will actually experience your inner knowing. You will perceive the world in a whole new way. And you will finally come to remember the truth of who you are: joyous, intuitive, loving and free.

1-56718-334-4, 240 pp., 6 x 9, softbound **$12.00**

Prices subject to change without notice.

THE SECRET OF LETTING GO
by Guy Finley

Whether you need to let go of a painful heartache, a destructive habit, a frightening worry or a nagging discontent, *The Secret of Letting Go* shows you how to call upon your own hidden powers and how they can take you through and beyond any challenge or problem. This book reveals the secret source of a brand-new kind of inner strength.

In the light of your new and higher self-understanding, emotional difficulties such as loneliness, fear, anxiety and frustration fade into nothingness as you happily discover they never really existed in the first place.

With a foreword by Desi Arnaz Jr., and introduction by Dr. Jesse Freeland, *The Secret of Letting Go* is a pleasing balance of questions and answers, illustrative examples, truth tales, and stimulating dialogues that allow the reader to share in the exciting discoveries that lead up to lasting self-liberation.

This is a book for the discriminating, intelligent, and sensitive reader who is looking for real answers.

0-87542-223-3, 240 pp., 5¼ x 8, softcover **$9.95**

WOMEN'S PSYCHIC LIVES
by Diane Stein

This book is a comprehensive course in psychic understanding, and ends women's psychic isolation forever. It contains the theory and explanation of psychic phenomena, women's shared and varied experiences, and how-to material for every woman's growth and psychic development. The reclamation of being psychic is women's reclamation of Goddess—and of their Goddess Being.

That reclaiming of women's psychic abilities and psychic lives is a major issue in Goddess spirituality and in the wholeness of women. Learning that everyone is psychic, learning what the phenomena mean, sharing and understanding others' experiences, and learning how to develop women's own abilities is information women are ready and waiting for in this dawning Age of Aquarius and Age of Women.

In the Greek legends of Troy, Cassandra, daughter of Hecuba, was gifted with prophecy. She gained her gift as a child at Delphi when she Stroked the Pythons of Gaea's temple, becoming a psychic priestess. Gaea, the Python, was the Goddess of oracles and mother/creator of the Earth.

In this book are fascinating accounts of women's psychic experiences. Learn how to develop your own, natural psychic abilities through the extensive advice given in Stroking the Python.

0-87542-757-X, 381 pp., 6 x 9, illus., softcover **$12.95**

Prices subject to change without notice.

SECRETS OF A NATURAL MENOPAUSE
A Positive, Drug-Free Approach
by Edna Copeland Ryneveld

Negotiate your menopause without losing your health, your sanity, or your integrity! *Secrets of a Natural Menopause* provides you with simple, natural treatments—using herbs, vitamins and minerals, foods, homeopathy, yoga, and meditation—that are safer (and cheaper) than estrogen replacement therapy.

Simply turn to the chapter describing the treatment you're interested in and look up any symptom from arthritis, depression, and hair loss to osteoporosis and varicose veins—you'll find time-honored as well as modern methods of preventing or alleviating menopausal symptoms that work, all described in plain, friendly language you won't need a medical dictionary to understand.

For years, allopathic medicine has treated menopause as a disease brought on by a deficiency of hormones instead of a perfectly natural transition. *Secrets of a Natural Menopause* will help you discover what's best for your body and empower you to take control of your own health and well-being.

1-56718-596-7, 224 pp., 6 x 9, illus. **$12.95**

THE ULTIMATE CURE
The Healing Energy Within You
by Dr. Jim Dreaver

The Ultimate Cure will open a door into consciousness and literally bring you into a direct, first-hand experience of illumination—an experience that will stimulate your mind, warm your heart and feed your soul.

Dr. Jim Dreaver provides a first-hand account of the spiritual journey and outlines the steps needed to live in the world with an authentic sense of wisdom, love and power. He addresses the issues of meditation, work as a spiritual exercise, harnessing the power of the mind, conscious breathing, and healing the wounds of the past. Dr. Dreaver's main theme is that spiritual presence, which is the source of all healing, is an actual, palpable reality that can be felt and tapped into.

To realize enlightenment, you must have a tremendous hunger for it. This delightfully honest and wonderfully human book will stimulate your appetite and, by the time you turn to the last page, will leave you feeling totally satisfied.

1-56718-244-5, 288 pp., 6 x 9, softcover **$14.95**

Prices subject to change without notice.

SENSUOUS LIVING
Expand Your Sensory Awareness
by Nancy Conger

Take a wonderful journey into the most intense source of delight and pleasure humans can experience: the senses! Enjoying your sense of sight, sound, smell, taste and touch is your birthright. Learn to treasure it with this guide to sensuous living.

Most of us revel in our senses unabashedly as children, but societal norms gradually train us to be too busy or disconnected from ourselves to savor them fully. By intentionally practicing sensuous ways of living, you can regain the art of finding beauty and holiness in simple things. This book provides activities to help you engage fully in life through your senses. Relish the touch of sun-dried sheets on your skin. Tantalize your palate with unusual foods and taste your favorites with a new awareness. Attune to tiny auditory pleasures that surround you, from the click of computer keys to raindrops hitting a window. Appreciate light, shadow and color with an artist's eye.

Revel in the sensory symphony that surrounds you and live more fully. Practice the fun techniques in this book and heighten every moment of your life more—you're entitled!

1-56718-160-0, 224 pp., 6x9, illus., softcover **$12.95**

CREATE YOUR OWN JOY
A Guide for Transforming Your Life
by Elizabeth Jean Rogers

Uncover the wisdom, energy and love of your higher self and discover the peace and joy for which you yearn! This highly structured journal-workbook is designed to guide you through the process of understanding how you create your own joy by how you choose to respond to people and situations in your life.

Each chapter offers guided meditations on overcoming blocks—such as guilt, grief, fear and destructive behavior—that keep happiness from you; thoughtful questions to help you focus your feelings; concrete suggestions for action; and affirmations to help you define and fulfill your deepest desires and true needs. As you record your responses to the author's questions, you will transform this book into a personal expression of your own experience.

Life is too short to waste your energy on negative thoughts and emotions—use the uncomplicated, dynamic ideas in this book to get a fresh outlook on current challenges in your life, and open the door to your joyful higher self.

1-56718-354-9, 240 pp., 6 x 9, illus., softcover **$10.00**

Prices subject to change without notice.

MAIDEN, MOTHER, CRONE
The Myth and Reality of the Triple Goddess
by D. J. Conway

The Triple Goddess is with every one of us each day of our lives. In our inner journeys toward spiritual evolution, each woman and man goes through the stages of Maiden (infant to puberty), Mother (adult and parent) and Crone (aging elder). *Maiden, Mother, Crone* is a guide to the myths and interpretations of the Great Goddess archetype and her three faces, so that we may better understand and more peacefully accept the cycle of birth and death.

Learning to interpret the symbolic language of the myths is important to spiritual growth, for the symbols are part of the map that guides each of us to the Divine Center. Through learning the true meaning of the ancient symbols, through facing the cycles of life, and by following the meditations and simple rituals provided in this book, women and men alike can translate these ancient teachings into personal revelations.

Not all goddesses can be conveniently divided into the clear aspects of Maiden, Mother and Crone. This book covers these as well, including the Fates, the Muses, Valkyries and others.

0-87542-171-7, 240 pp., 6 x 9, softcover **$12.95**

THE COMPLETE HANDBOOK OF NATURAL HEALING
by Marcia Starck

Got an itch that won't go away? Want a massage but don't know the difference between Rolfing, Reichian Therapy and Reflexology? Tired of going to the family doctor for minor illnesses that you know you could treat at home—if you just knew how?

Designed to function as a home reference guide (yet enjoyable and interesting enough to be read straight through), this book addresses all natural healing modalities in use today: dietary regimes, nutritional supplements, cleansing and detoxification, vitamins and minerals, herbology, homeopathic medicine and cell salts, traditional Chinese medicine, Ayurvedic medicine, body work therapies, exercise, mental and spiritual therapies, and more. In addition, a section of 41 specific ailments outlines natural treatments for everything from acne to varicose veins.

0-87542-742-1, 416 pp., 6 x 9, softcover **$12.95**

Prices subject to change without notice.

DESIGNING YOUR OWN DESTINY
The Power to Shape Your Future
by Guy Finley

This book is for those who are ready for a book on self-transformation with principles that actually work. *Designing Your Own Destiny* is a practical, powerful guide that tells you, in plain language, exactly what you need to do to fundamentally change yourself and your life for the better, permanently.

Eleven powerful inner life exercises will show you how to master the strong and subtle forces that actually determine your life choices and your destiny. You'll discover why so many of your daily choices up to this point have been made by default, and how embracing the truth about yourself will banish your self-defeating behaviors forever. Everything you need for spiritual success is revealed in this book. Guy Finley reveals and removes many would-be roadblocks to your inner transformation, telling you how to dismiss fear, cancel self-wrecking resentment, stop secret self-sabotage and stop blaming others for the way you feel.

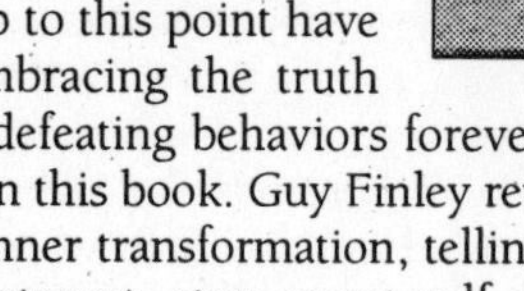

After reading *Designing Your Own Destiny*, you'll understand why you are perfectly equal to every task you set for yourself, and that you truly can change your life for the better!

1-56718-278-X, 160 pp., mass market, softcover **$6.99**

DREAMS & WHAT THEY MEAN TO YOU
by Migene Gonzalez Wippler

Everyone dreams. Yet dreams are rarely taken seriously—they seem to be only a bizarre series of amusing or disturbing images that the mind creates for no particular purpose. Yet dreams, through a language of their own, contain essential information about ourselves which, if properly analyzed and understood, can change our lives. In this fascinating and well-written book, the author gives you all of the information needed to begin interpreting—even creating—your own dreams.

Dreams & What They Mean To You begins by exploring the nature of the human mind and consciousness, then discusses the results of the most recent scientific research on sleep and dreams. The author analyzes different types of dreams: telepathic, nightmares, sexual and prophetic. In addition, there is an extensive Dream Dictionary which lists the meanings for a wide variety of dream images.

Most importantly, Gonzalez-Wippler tells you how to practice creative dreaming—consciously controlling dreams as you sleep. Once a person learns to control his dreams, his horizons will expand and his chances of success will increase!

0-87542-288-8, 240 pp., mass market **$3.95**

Prices subject to change without notice.